Concrete Universality

Concrete Universality

Philosophy for an Age of Fragmentation

LORENZO MARSILI

polity

First published in 2027 by Polity Press Ltd.

Polity Press Ltd.
65 Bridge Street
Cambridge CB2 1UR, UK

Polity Press Ltd.
111 River Street
Hoboken, NJ 07030, USA

ISBN-13: 978-1-5095-7622-7
ISBN-13: 978-1-5095-7623-4(pb)

A catalogue record for this book is available from the British Library.

Library of Congress Control Number: 2026936735

Typeset in 11 on 14pt Warnock Pro
by Cheshire Typesetting Ltd, Cuddington, Cheshire
Printed and bound in Great Britain by Ashford Colour Ltd

For further information on Polity, visit our website: politybooks.com

Contents

You must know, Sancho, that all the things that happen to us have to do with enchantments, and that in the life of knights-errant everything depends upon them; and so what seems to you a barber's basin seems to me the helmet of Mambrino, and to others it will seem something else again.

Don Quixote

Introduction: Of Nations and Truths

The last three centuries have represented a unique historical aberration. For the first time in the history of the world, and probably for the last, the interpretation and transformation of our planet in the widest sense – from the history of its peoples to the alteration of its climate – was determined by events and ways of thinking taking shape in a narrow and culturally homogeneous part of it: the Asian peninsula called Europe and its American offspring. Today, we witness the closure of this eccentricity.

More profoundly, the past five thousand years have been characterized by the human monopoly over writing and over the search for and generation of truth. Today, we witness the challenge to that monopoly as advances in predictive algorithms and artificial intelligence collapse reality into computed artefacts.

What becomes of universal truth and values in an age of geopolitical and algorithmic fragmentation?

The end of universalism

As you enter St Peter's Square in Rome, you are embraced by the monumental colonnade built by Gian Lorenzo Bernini, one of the Baroque's greatest sculptors and architects. The columns depart from the central basilica as a pair of embracing elliptical arms that welcome and contain you. Here is the church accepting you into the universal faith, whoever you may be and wherever you may come from.

Never satisfied, the eternal city has played capital to two universal beliefs. Just as everyone could become an equal member of the Christian congregation on condition of recognizing the truth of the Gospel, so could anyone benefit from the protection of the Roman Empire and its citizenship rights provided they accepted the primacy of Roman law.[1]

On the other side of the Eurasian continent, the Forbidden City in Beijing presents significant architectural similarities to the ideas materialized by Bernini in Rome. The monumental courtyard facing the first pavilion of the imperial palace served to welcome and astonish representatives from China's world as they arrived in Beijing to pay tribute to the emperor and comply with the required rites.

Both Roman and Chinese civilizations referred to themselves as the whole world. Imperial Rome was *caput orbis terrarum*, or the capital of the world, while the Chinese imperial palace was the centre of *Tianxia*, or all under heaven. Anyone existing outside their political, cultural and religious influence was literally living outside the civilized universe. And so, both left ample space of autonomy for the plurality of states, ethnicities and religions they presided over, while internal tolerance for diversity was mirrored by a lenient disdain for the existence of life outside the empire.[2]

Modern European imperialism, on the other hand, was *total*. It was characterized by the rule of one nation over the others, and it was the weight of that nation's total way of life that was imposed on the conquered.[3]

As decolonial and postcolonial thought has amply discussed, European imperialism did not merely impose military conquest, economic dominion or political control. It was not anchored simply in the hierarchical relation of different cultures and the extraction of value from the periphery to the centre; it was, much more profoundly, the transformation of European particularism – its singular mode of existing and interpreting reality – into the only universally valid and valuable form of life.[4]

To understand the depth and psychological impact of such imposition, a European or American reader should imagine that power had flown the other way – and that, say, China had taken Europe's mantle. In the span of a mere few decades, Europe would be commanded and then forced to give up its Greek and Christian philosophical and religious heritage, relinquishing concepts such as those of *polis* and *demos*, of law and liberty, and ultimately brushing aside its entire intellectual armoury from Parmenides to Kant, replacing its foundational concepts for unheard-of Chinese notions that would now represent the only embodiment of intellectual civility. Meanwhile, Europeans would witness the reduction of their history to mere local folklore. The French Revolution, for instance, would no longer represent a world-historical event, but an insignificant peasant rebellion in a backward province. The history of China would become the singular incarnation of the universal spirit of History.

Geopolitical enlightenment

In his landmark *Prison Notebooks*, written while in isolation in a fascist jail in the 1920s, Italian Marxist philosopher Antonio Gramsci presents a very brief discussion of Immanuel Kant's famous categorical imperative: 'Act only according to that maxim whereby you can at the same time will that it should become a universal law.' With no access to primary sources, and writing from memory, Gramsci misquotes Kant and rephrases the sentence in this way: 'Act in such a way that your conduct can become a norm for all men *in similar conditions*.'[5] Understandably, Gramsci would then go on to ask: What is meant by similar conditions? He concludes that Kant's maxim presupposes a single culture, a single religion, a worldwide conformism, and that Kant is ultimately only able to speak to and morally bind people like him: cosmopolitan European intellectuals.

Gramsci asked of Kant the same question that Friedrich Nietzsche would pose of the metaphysics of truth: *Who speaks?* Where Kant repeatedly postulates the existence of a common sense or judgement shared by all and forming the basis for cosmopolitan understanding, Gramsci and Nietzsche, and later critical theory and postcolonial thought, would ask: Whose common sense is this? Whose particularity is this claim to universality? What is the process that has led to its rise and that sustains its hegemony?

Gramsci first provincializes Europe,[6] underscoring how Kant's universalism was factually sustained by very particular infrastructures such as the emergence of the bourgeois public sphere, the circulation of print culture or the stability afforded by the modern state. Gramsci's misquotation is today representative of a generalized spirit of the age.

An air of freedom breathes across the world as the provincialization of the West leads to a rediscovery and celebration of civilizational particularity. From Beijing to Kigali, universal European values are seen only to apply to 'men of similar conditions' and to represent 'a single culture' that extended no further than the gunboats defending it. With waning military and economic domination, European and American claims to universality are denuded as a particularity, their 'worldwide conformism' as a violent imposition. Now that formerly colonized countries have succeeded in curtailing the reach of Western imposition, they are free to indulge in the prized fruit of liberty: shaping their worldview with reference to their own tradition.

The effects are shattering, politically as much as philosophically. Well beyond geopolitics, it is a deeply embedded conception of the world, of truth and of meaning that is upset by the unchaining of the rest of the world. Not only is Europe's own universalist inclination shown to be historically hypocritical, self-interested and perennially betrayed, but the very aspiration to universal truths, values and rights is demoted to mere particularistic preference in a world where *only particularities exist.*

The rise of multipolarity and the recuperation of an autonomous speaking voice for much of the world represents not merely the end of empire in the political, or *imperial*, sense but more profoundly in its logical, or *imperative*, formulation.

Immanuel Kant understood freedom as autonomy: the ability to bind ourselves (*autos*) by norms (*nomos*) of our own making. Autonomy implies self-determination. And that is why it would be a mistake to read today's particularistic or civilizational turn as mere nationalism or revanchism. It is, rather, a form of *enlightenment.*

As is well known, Kant defines enlightenment as a process that releases humanity from a status of immaturity. Immaturity is in turn defined as accepting someone else's authority where the use of autonomous reason would be called for. Immatures are those who rely on a book, a priest or a doctor to tell them what to think, believe or eat. Enlightenment is the process by which individuals replace heteronomous authorities with their own autonomous faculties of critical reflection. And so, to the extent that much of the world, until very recently, was kept in a condition of immaturity by a Western overseer, the ongoing rejection of Western tutelage and the ensuing emancipation may be understood as a form of *geopolitical enlightenment*, whereby a plurality of human communities envision contributing first hand to the determination of their futures. Western kings, doctors and priests – nations, technology and civilization – lose the power to delimit and determine their space of manoeuvre.

Paradoxically, the planetary redistribution of the spirit of the Enlightenment corners and debunks the Enlightenment's own celebration of universal values and truths and its categorical moral and philosophical implications.

If the West is dead, all is allowed

The impact of colonialism on the colonized has been the object of academically rich, politically powerful and morally significant research. But the cognitive and philosophical effects *on the Western mind* of the waning of Western domination over the planet are underestimated.[7]

A defining characteristic of ideology is its invisibility to the bearer. Like the frame of a pair of spectacles that is made to disappear by the accustomed brain of the wearer, like a well-fitting pair of shoes that our feet no longer notice, so Europeans and North Americans were overall oblivious to the exceptionality of their position in the world as they studied the planet through the lenses of their particularist universalism and trampled over it with their hobnailed boots. But now the spectacles are broken, and the eyes notice the plaster on the frames. The shoes have come apart at the seams.[8]

French phenomenologist Maurice Merleau-Ponty famously pointed out that a stick literally disappears for a blind man, transforming from an object of investigation to an extension of subjectivity. Similarly, the lenses of hegemony have served to expand and augment Europe's perception, literally dilating its being-in-the-world. But once the lenses fracture and return to be perceived as an object, then one looks not through them but at them, noticing their texture and questioning the processes that supported their fabrication.

Emmanuel Levinas's empathic moral philosophy rotates around the encounter with 'the face of the Other.' It has inspired decolonial thought, such as Enrique Dussel's theology of liberation. And yet, Levinas unwittingly shows to what extent the dislocation of a European centre shakes the Western mind. While discussing the rising claims for civilizational particularism in the context of decolonization, he belittles them as a saraband of innumerable and equivalent cultures, each justifying itself in its own context. In *Humanisme de l'autre homme,* he points out that such celebration of particularity would, with a cunning play on words, lead to a world at the same time *désoccidentalisé* and *désorienté,* or disoccidentalized and (hence) disoriented. A world without a *grounding* is a world out of joint, one of contingency and arbitrariness. It is a malfunctioning compass that no longer has a North.

There is, of course, a deeper philosophical explanation for this view. And it is that the perceived threat of *relativism* as all stable Being is replaced by the incessant flow of context-dependent becoming. As Souleymane Bachir Diagne has underlined,[9] Levinas is really taking aim at anti-Platonic or postmetaphysical philosophy, wishing to preserve a conception of truth as transcending all particular languages and cultures used to express it. Even where Levinas wished to substitute, with another clever word play, *l'être* for *l'autre,* or Being for the Other, the opposite of European universalism is seen to be particularistic nihilism as 'the modern expression of atheism'.[10] This is the world of Platonic geopolitics, with the One necessarily grounding the Many.

What happens then when the One withers away? Enlightenment calls for the use of autonomous faculties of reason. But if universal reason is replaced with a myriad of incommensurable traditions and interests, then the perceived risk is a refraction of truth *and reason* into a thousand individualized statements valid no longer than for the short span of their enunciation.

Cuius regio, eius religio – whose realm, their religion – was the maxim crafted in 1555 to end the German wars of religion and ultimately enshrine the principle of national sovereignty. *Cuius regio, eius veritas* may become the standard of geopolitical enlightenment – whose civilization, their truth. A world fragmented across large spaces that organize and command their internal plurality while stopping short of attempting to organize or command the internal life of other blocs in a generalized absence of any overarching orientation.

If God is dead, then all is permitted. Such was the terror that haunted the European mind at the close of the nineteenth century as it broke free of the certainties of religion, progress and truth. Today's psychology presents a geopolitical paraphrase of Europe's encounter with the daemon of nihilism: if the West is dead, then all is allowed.

Borges' paradox

The trial of European universalism might recall that of Otto Dietrich, the fictional Nazi commander imagined by Jorge Luis Borges in 'Deutsches Requiem'. As he is tried in Nuremberg, Dietrich unexpectedly claims victory for Germany. The Allies may have won the war, he argues, but to do so they have had to transform themselves into a machine as ruthless as the Third Reich. Germany went under, but the new man it stood for prevailed and conquered the conquerors. With his classical taste for paradox, Borges provides a chilling reminder that we can lose in victory if we let ourselves become a mirror image of our opponent.

Similarly, civilizational particularism risks condoning the very actions it sets out to critique. Ultimately, Emmanuel

Levinas was not *simply* representing a European nostalgia for a world that made sense *to Europeans*. He was, at the same time, issuing a warning of wider relevance: if we relinquish all grounding, reduce universal values to a proxy of Western interest and accept that any culture can justify itself on its own grounds, then all that we have left is the logic of power. Might makes right, as moral absolutes and a-contextual truths are debunked as always already *someone's* morals and truths. This logic, in an echo of the Aristotelian confutation of relativism, would ultimately short-circuit the original condemnation of Western oppression itself. If all is permitted, then the West cannot be blamed for having ruthlessly pursued its own wealth and power.

This is a deeper intellectual paradox running through much critical and emancipatory contemporary philosophy. Whether it is postcolonial and decolonial thought opening onto a world of pluriversality, or the genealogical unmaking of class, race and gender-speaking positions, or more generally the celebration of difference, multiplicity and ontological plurality, one question remains unanswered: *why* should any of these positions be preferable to their opposite? What is it that *grounds* the thought of equality and plurality, as opposed to, with Thucydides, accepting that the strong do what they can and the weak suffer what they must?

Cuius algorithmus, eius veritas

The cacophony of a world liberated from a centre plays its dissonant notes all around us. It is the stuff of geopolitical confusion, of questioned identities and existential disorientation. But it is also, quite concretely, the multiplication of noise through the acceleration of information technology, the splintering of communication in the time of social media, the multiplication of artificially generated outputs that literally crowd out any principle of orientation. Dissonance is incarnated in the infrastructures of our time.

Few things signal the multiple refraction of the One into the Many better than scientific advance on predictive algorithms. For the first time, truth is not only contested but computed. What was once the privilege of metaphysics or divine revelation has become the output of an algorithmic process, a product of mathematical training rather than a claimed correspondence with reality. Artificial intelligence does not possess a universal concept of truth. It operates instead through the calibration of probabilities, optimizing correlations across vast fields of data. What we call a true result is, in fact, the most statistically consistent one – the pattern that best satisfies the model's internal logic, not necessarily the one that reveals the world as it supposedly is. There is, furthermore, an original institutional choice at the level of the enabling conditions concerning a model's statistical structure, or its architecture and training, and there is a further and more explicit institutional choice concerning the protocols employed, or the conditions of appearance, circulation and operational reality of the model's internal distinctions.

Truth is not discovered but generated. Truth is an artefact. Literally, a work of art.

This shift marks a profound philosophical mutation. The conditions of truth are no longer external to production, but are encoded within the machinery of calculation itself. Every dataset, model or optimization criterion constructs a micro-world of truth, a domain in which meaning is internally coherent but potentially incommensurable with others. As systems become more autonomous, their internal criteria of verification may evolve beyond human comprehension, inaugurating an era in which truth exists and thrives without us.

In this new epistemic order, the Enlightenment dream of a single, shared rationality gives way to a landscape of algorithmic sovereignties. Each computational architecture carries its own *logos*, its own grammar of verification and error. We are, in a sense, entering a world of philosophical *laissez-faire*: no longer governed by universal values, rights or truths capable of orienting the totality, but by the shifting hierarchies of machine-generated plausibility. The very question of truth now depends on who controls the code, who trains the model, who defines the loss function that regulates what counts as 'accuracy.'

Cuius algorithmus, eius veritas – whose algorithm, their truth.

Protocols of truth

To grasp what is at stake, we must descend beneath the level of truth as a computed output and examine the very conditions under which anything can appear to be an artificial system in the first place. For these new regimes of truth-production arise not only from the variability of datasets or the opacity of neural architectures, but from the basic operations through which the world is segmented and made computationally legible. Before an algorithm can ever declare something true, it must decide what a thing is. This is the first and most consequential act: the individuation of units, the carving of linguistic or visual continuities into discrete elements capable of being manipulated. Tokenization, often treated as a negligible preprocessing step, is in fact a metaphysical intervention, or a culturally contingent decision about the grain of reality. It presupposes that meaning is composed of discrete, combinable units; that language is a sequence of parts rather than a flow; that the world can be modularized. Entire ontologies are foreclosed or privileged at this primordial cut.

From these initial units of meaning, models build internal architectures of relation – latent geometries in which concepts acquire position, weight and potential. Yet this internal individuation remains inert without the procedures that determine what may surface and in what form. Protocols – ranging from input formats to safety layers, API schemas and institutional workflows – regulate every passage from internal structure to external appearance.

This tension between latent structure and governed appearance is constitutive. It defines the condition of contemporary artificial systems, in which the production of distinctions, meanings and truths is inseparable from the institutional protocols that mediate them. A model's internal structure determines what it could say and a protocol determines what it is allowed to say. With every cycle of training, finetuning and feedback – each governed by normative choices about what to store, what to discard and what to label as 'good' and hence 'true' – the system's *being* is reshaped once again in a recursive circuit of ontological production. The generation of truth today is inseparable from the creation of what used to be called Being or essence and that was thought to forever and immutably be.

Ontopoiesis

If we wished to draw a caricature of European philosophy, we could do worse than sketch a portrait of god.

European thought has circled obsessively around the search for what endures behind what passes. From Plato's forms to Aristotle's substances, from the medieval *ens realissimum* to the modern Subject, thought has sought a ground and a stable anchor that could arrest the flux of appearances and guarantee reality.

This desire for permanence has generated a dual world. On the one hand stands the realm of becoming: the fleeting, deceptive and ephemeral; on the other, the perfect sphere of Being: the true, real and eternal. The wedge driven between these two orders shapes the Western conception of reality itself, consigning the becoming of lived immediacy to the status of illusion, and reserving truth for an abstract domain beyond it.

The European penchant for intellectual abstraction deserves full honours. The quest for the ideal and the denudement of mere reality in favour of its hidden truth have constituted an explosive engine of progress: the double revolution that inaugurated modernity – industrial and French, scientific and political – owes it no small debt. Searching for Being – for the ultimate essential nature of things – proved spectacularly fruitful even if the object of inquiry was all along an illusion. Just like Christopher Columbus, one searches for India and stumbles upon America.

But today this voyage of discovery is no longer productive of the future. The withering away of Western hegemony, coupled with the emergent right of intellectual invention for multiple traditions and for artificial intelligence, may finally free the West itself from its addiction to stability and grounding. In this sense, contemporary geopolitical Enlightenment may succeed where the eighteenth-century European variety failed, finally freeing the mind from god.

In the pages that follow, we will foster an inclination, or a way of perception, that will lead us to understand ontology not as the *logos* of the *ontos*, or the science of Being, but *ontopoiesis*, or the incessant creation (*poiesis*) of reality and of that which *is*.

Ontopoiesis is the name for the new regime of worldmaking in which human, natural and artificial systems participate. A regime in which the distinction between what exists and what appears collapses into a generative entanglement. A regime in which the metaphysical assumptions of AI tokenization, the normative force of protocols, the authority of institutions and the freedom of human art and politics together determine what may count as a thing, an event, a claim or a truth.

This will be, of course, the very opposite of the type of metaphysical and moral realism that grounds absolutes, truths and universals. It will be, on the contrary, the closest one can get to justifying that *anything goes* and all is equally allowed. And yet, it will be precisely such a conception of ontological creation that will lead us to formulate a new conception of universality for a fragmented world – where universality is a byname for the kind of *truths* that have a force that everyone must behold.

We will begin by investigating the ontological effects of geopolitical Enlightenment. In the first chapter – dialoguing across European, Chinese and Indian philosophies, quantum mechanics and artificial intelligence – we will explore the idea that truth does not pre-exist an engagement with reality, and that the transformation of reality transforms, or rather forms, truth. We will then scout around for a new organizing principle for a splintered world, reimagining, in the second chapter, universality for the age of geopolitical Enlightenment. This will lead us to collapse the distinction between what something *is* and what it *does*, underscoring the primacy of the political act. Finally, in the conclusion we will gesture towards a concrete, political application of such reworked conception of universality and truth. A word of methodological caution: we will proceed in circular and not linear fashion – by accumulation, resonance and association, returning to and expanding the same concepts throughout the pages.

This is a work of metaphysics. And hence, as we will demonstrate, of politics.

Ontopoiesis

The origins

If one philosopher may lay claim to having established a foundational dichotomy that would influence the entire history of Western thought, that is probably Parmenides of Elea, born in the late sixth century BCE in a Greek colony in southern Italy.

While many of his contemporaries tried to uncover the structure of the universe – for instance, discussing whether it was made of air, fire or water – Parmenides placed the accent on what all these suppositions shared: the fact that whether the world is made up of water or fire, Democritean atoms or Pythagorean numerical harmony, each and every one of these things must first and foremost *be*. Hence it is nothing but *Being* that lies at the heart of the universe and that pervades all things.

This mesmerizing thought – which would first establish *ontology*, or the study of Being – is the foundational abstraction that would haunt and define European philosophical and religious thought for millennia to come. After Parmenides, the Greek, European and, ultimately, Western mind would forever oscillate between foundationalism and relativism, between the search for that which immutably *is* and the despair that no such thing may ever surrender itself to the human mind.

With the incorporation of Romanized Judaism into the Roman Empire and its hybridization with Greek philosophy, the thought of Being would provide the cardinal points for Christian theology: the death of god is the death of Being and the death of Being that of god.

Truth, too, would become inseparable from Being. The fragments that remain of Parmenides' writing draw an essential distinction: that between truth and opinion – *aletheia* and *doxa*. The former elevates us to knowledge of the absolute. The latter leaves us lingering in a world of flickering shadows. The world splits in two. In its many and successful iterations over the course of millennia, this would become the foundational distinction separating that which *essentially is* from that which *merely appears*: truth from illusion, the immutable from the changeable, Being from becoming.

Of course, one of the most renowned images of Greek philosophy speaks directly to this distinction. Captive men, chained in a damp hollow cave, observe like mesmerized children the play of shadows projected on the walls by the glow of the fire. The objects lying *behind* and *causing* the shadows remain outside their view. Shadows are all they know to be real. Until one among them is freed, stands up, turns his back on his fellow inmates and walks towards daylight. And there, from the fissure in the rock, beckons the world in all its splendour. 'That is the real world!', he shouts to his companions, 'Turn around!' He exhorts them to stand up, turn their back to the puppet theatre and see reality as it *truly is*.

Our unfortunate primitive philosopher is ridiculed for that. And yet, from that moment on, living up to his legacy will become the task of nearly every European philosopher: to turn humans away from the *particular*, with its vagaries and uncertainties, and towards the *universal*; away from the pettiness of the *concrete*, and towards the aristocracy of the *abstract*. The object of philosophical inquiry, that eternal question that for Aristotle has always puzzled and disoriented, would become none other than the nature of 'Being qua Being'[1] or the being of Being. Philosophers search after *ousia*, pure existence, also translated as substance, and defined as something not existing particularly, a *particular* being, but something existing absolutely.

Aristotle distinguishes between what is said 'relative to another' and what is said 'in itself'.[2] Where relative beings exist only through reference to something else, intrinsic beings possess independent, essential reality. Nearly the entire history of European philosophy could be described as the search for reality in a world of shadows.

In the *Theaetetus*, Plato contrasts the philosopher's life with the life of the litigious man of the law courts. Philosophers do not busy themselves with ephemeral human affairs. Rather, they direct their soul towards what is eternal. By setting their gaze on Being, philosophers free themselves from the turmoil and flux of Becoming. They live contemplatively, aiming to align their character with the unchanging order of the cosmos. This alignment allows them to become 'like god as far as possible',[3] founding their existence on immutable forms rather than on the transient world of change.

It was a disciple of Parmenides and fellow inhabitant of southern Italy, Zeno of Elea, who would draw out of his teacher's quest for Being the *law of contradiction*. This is the idea that something cannot *be* and *not be* at the same time. Logically, two contradictory statements cannot be true at the same time; we cannot say that the fire both is and is not hot. Ontologically, no single thing can at the same time both possess and not possess a certain property; the fire, quite independently of what anyone says, cannot actually be both hot and not hot.

From this principle a separate but correlate foundational dichotomy of Greek and hence European thought would emerge: the *principle of the excluded middle*, stating that either something *is* or it *is not*. The fire is either hot or it is not hot, and no third option exists. It could certainly be lukewarm, but then it *is not* hot.

These principles would provide the tools for the primordial defence of Being against the attacks of scepticism and relativism – the thought, that is, that *only shadows exist* and hence nothing inherently *is* (true) but everything merely *appears* to a particular spectator looking from a particular angle.

Let us imagine, argues Aristotle in *The Metaphysics*, that somebody wished to oppose the law of non-contradiction. Our opponent could not deny the law without at the same time assuming its validity. Their conviction about the validity of their own relativist enunciation would undermine their own view and confirm that indeed some things are (true) and others are not. If, however, they coherently held to the principle that nothing ultimately is (true), but that all can both be and not be at the same time and in the same way, they would then have to admit that their own relativist position would be equally valid to the opposite opinion, thereby plunging their argument into non-sense. Relativists, so the traditional confutation goes, are either forced to betray their own enunciation or remain silent. This is quite directly what Aristotle tells us: if humans renounce the principle of non-contradiction, they are reduced to the condition of plants.[4]

Something either is or it is not. It cannot *both* be and not be; and it cannot *neither* be nor not be. Western languages operate grammatically and conceptually around this very dichotomous or *dilemmic* principle, narrowing the space for the enunciation of any way out. You literally cannot speak unless you accept this departing point of Greek philosophy.[5]

Mourning the withdrawal of Being

The European Enlightenment first establishes incredulity towards reality as the sentiment of the modern age. It is with Immanuel Kant that access to the absolute or immutable comes to be generally accepted as something *mediated* by subjectivity. Space, time and causality, for instance, are not properties of the world existing independently, but categories that enable us to relate to it and that shape our perception of it. This *correlational* framework implies that the *objective* is always mediated by *subjective* conditions, and any knowledge of the external world is inseparable from the mind's structuring principles and hence ultimately unknowable in its autonomous essence. We have no direct access to Being, but always merely stretch towards it with the clumsy prosthesis of our thoughts and senses.

The prosthesis is a duplicitous medication, reminiscent of the *pharmakon* that is at once cure and poison. It enables us to lean towards Being, but it wraps us so tight that our skin cannot touch it: we cannot grasp the *thing-in-itself* – the way anything *really is* outside its contingent relation to an observer – but only the *thing-for-us*, the way it manifests itself to our sensitivity.

Our senses operate like the medicine that would not leave the body spoken by the Buddha: 'Kasyapa, if a physician gives his patient some medicine to purge an illness, but the medicine stays in the body instead of being discharged, what do you think? Will the patient get better? No, World-Honoured One. The patient's illness will become worse if the medicine is not discharged.'[6]

Our mind turns into Plato's cave. We are inmates of an intractable penitentiary who are permanently denied access to the great outdoors of reality. We can never step outside our human perspective to access a world unfiltered by our consciousness or interpretive frameworks, our senses or our histories, our languages or our social and cultural structures. And so it is only the categories that govern our thought processes that we may inquire about and discover. The whole point of critique, from its Kantian origin to the present,[7] is precisely to subtract that which *is not* so as to uncover that *which is*, however feeble that may be. Until precisely the unknowability of Being becomes its only guarantee: reality exists, in-itself, even if *we* cannot know it, and it exists *precisely because* we can know that we cannot know it. The famous concluding lines of Wittgenstein's *Tractatus Logico-Philosophicus* – 'Whereof one cannot speak, thereof one must be silent' – say literally this: we cannot speak of that which lies beyond language, but we can and do speak of our inability to speak of *it* (and so – *it*, are you there?).

Jorge Luis Borges has beautifully captured this condition in his poem 'The Other Tiger':

> Let us look for a third tiger. This one
> will be a form in my dream like all the others,
> a system, an arrangement of human language,
> and not the flesh-and-bone tiger
> that, out of reach of all mythologies,
> paces the earth. I know all this; yet something
> drives me to this ancient, perverse adventure,
> foolish and vague, yet still I keep on looking
> throughout the evening for the other tiger,
> the other tiger, the one not in this poem.[8]

All the tigers I could think of will be just forms in the human dream of language. Tigers of a lesser kind, deprived of autonomy and inescapably enmeshed with my senses and mental states, tigers for-me and not in-themselves, dependent tigers, just *my* tigers, my beloved, particular tigers. And yet, something in us inclines to search for the *real* tiger, the one that would apply to all and whose existence no one could deny – the *universal* tiger, the one that you and I would *have* to see in the same way. That search is the perverse adventure, foolish and vague, that has shaped the Greek and European mind and its philosophical, political and legal history. This is the adventure that is reduced to the particular behaviour of an eccentric civilization by the epistemic impact of geopolitical Enlightenment.

Faust's *Was die Welt im Innersten zusammenhält*:

> That I may know what holds the world together
> in its inmost core,
> behold the driving force,
> and seed of all becoming,
> and no longer rummage in words.[9]

The history of modern philosophy may be described as the attempt to come to terms with the collapse of the Faustian aspiration. The reality we have access to is always conditioned and conditional, dependent-on, hence ultimately weak, not in-itself but for-us, and so likely to always become but never be – never be self-identical, never be essence, never be stable and hence never be god.

The European experience of living through the withdrawal of Being, the death of god and the collapse of certainty and stable truth has represented an intellectual drama and trauma of epic proportions, informing more than a century of philosophical, literary, theatrical, psychoanalytical and artistic production – from Dostoevsky to Beckett, from Zarathustra's descent from the mountain to Roquentin's nausea in the streets of Bouville.

The funeral of metaphysics leaves in its stead a memory and a mourning presence. The thing-in-itself is the amputated ghost limb of the European philosophical body. A structuring absence that can be seen to remain as a residue of thought even in the most anti-metaphysical philosophies[10] and that keeps European thought quite literally a monarchy: the rule (*arkhein*) of the missing One (*monos*).

万物: From Eros to the *monotopia*

Chinese philosophers, of course, never fell in love with a veiled ultimate reality.[11] And hence, they rarely fell prey to the despair of meaningless and nihilistic relativism. Generations of Chinese thinkers have developed a philosophical sensitivity that avoids declaring any one thing essentially true, and hence inherently superior to any other, without, however, declaring all things to be just the same.

As pre-Socratic philosopher Heraclitus pointed out in 500 BC, oppositions can exist only in reference to one another: they are inescapably symbiotic. We could not conceive the meaning of *hot* if we had no experience of *cold*; we could not grasp the sense of *day* if we had never seen *night*. Similarly, without a concept of Being, the meaning of becoming is itself transformed. Change is not the opposite of truth – that which transforms as opposed to that which is immutable. Appearance is not the opposite of essence – that which is fleeting as opposed to that which is eternal. And particularism is not the opposite of universalism.

While Nietzsche must forcefully brush aside the 'true world' he inherits from Platonic philosophy and from Christianity, while he must heroically and even violently extract it from the human mind, Chinese thought never relied on such wrestling with language to free it from the dominance of the ideal. The Chinese mind does not approach the liberated flow of life with the fatigued and exalted, traumatized and inebriated mind of the philosophical hero who traverses the desert of nihilism.

If Chinese philosophy never encounters the trauma of the subject's limited access to an in-itself, this is because it never possessed such a concept to begin with. We know that rather than *being*, it speaks of *having*, as Chinese language lacks a copulative sense of *to be* and rather uses the expression *you* (有), meaning *to have* or *to be present*. This results in the fact that anything that *is* must summon a particular *something* that contains it, as in the forest having trees, or the world having humans. Existence is always existence in a context – relational and situated.

As Roger Ames and David Hall explain: 'The distinction between the copulative sense of being as existing and the Chinese sense of being (*you*) as having turns out to be a difference between two modes of being present – the mediated and the unmediated. Mediated experience entails the fact that Being, in the mode of this or that essence, is made manifest through the particular beings of the world . . . Immediate experience requires that the particulars themselves are the objects of knowledge. Such particulars are grasped immediately in the sense that the experience of them is simply had.'[12]

Traditional concepts of mediation lead to objects existing twice: once as our perception of it, the other as in-itself (dangerous jungles: there are two tigers every time you say tiger). Ultimately, that which mediates – the prosthetic – takes over and becomes all we have direct access to. Mediation is the brewing ground for the withdrawal of and mourning for lost Being.

Non-mediated or immediate experience in the sense of something that *you* 有 does not imply the naive claim that we may access directly the one and only tiger, as in some pre-Kantian type of direct access to the thing-in-itself. This is, rather, an appeal not to theorize in the first instance the distinction between the thing-in-itself and the thing-for-us, or between Being and becoming – to disregard it, to shrug it off as an irrelevance. To be is quite simply to be around, to be available. The character 有 on the oracle bones is a hand holding a piece of meat, where the abstract idea is to have something to share with others.

An immediate relation is still a relation – *I* am not *that thing* – and in this sense there is still a *medium* that connects me and the thing that is there. This paradoxical immediacy of the medium may best be characterized as a *horizontal mediation.*

In Plato's *Symposium* the figure of Eros is introduced as a connector, and ultimately a mediator, between the perfect heaven of eternal Being and the mundane world of fleeting becoming. Priestess Diotima explains his position by referring to the concept of true opinion – an opinion that, given its truth, hits the mark of what really is, but which is not real knowledge as it cannot give explanations for its belief.[13] The vertical mediation of Eros serves to anchor the fleeting world of opinion onto the stability of Being. Eros literally pushes us up to stabilize and eternalize our discoveries. It is this erotic ecstasy for the absolute that would become enveloped in the prophylactic of Kantian categories and eventually be reduced to solipsistic auto-erotism.

But where Eros is a *vertical* mediator, the type of immediate relationality of classical Chinese philosophy is *horizontal,* remaining immanent to a singular plane of existence. *One place,* one world only, or a *monotopia,* that is not separated from anything else existing in some other, truer form and that we must erotically latch on to.

The transition from the *media* of legacy journalism to the unmediated flow of information on social media may provide an example. Traditional journalism actively creates the message as it narrates the event and connects that narration to the receiver of the information. Social media introduces a different type of mediating or *organizing* principle in the form of a substantial but flat algorithmic presence. Platforms stand in between the message of the content-creator and their audience and shape that encounter, organizing the way the message inhabits the flow of information: who receives it, how often, under what conditions. In doing so, they shape the message itself. They do so quite directly: once Facebook decided that posts containing videos would receive preferential algorithmic treatment, for instance, all newspapers began producing video content. And they shape the message contextually: the context in which a message appears, its *positioning* vis-à-vis other messages, may transform a sheer absurdity into a viral sensation and hence *change its being*, transforming that which it *is*. Here the mediation becomes horizontal; it is an immanent organizing principle that orients the *cartography* of the particulars in a specific *context* – it represents the shifting conditions that guide the encounter with the objects and thereby define them.

We may already signal here a similitude with contemporary *protocolism*, an emergent art form in which an artist designs a rule-set (a 'protocol') that guides or frames the creation or execution of works by other agents. The protocol defines the *environment* within which specific instantiations acquire their meaning. The *being* of an artwork lies not with *it* but with the wider context within which it operates. And this context can be *created*. We will have much more to say about this.

Similarly, in classical Chinese language, which operated without tenses, cases, genders or definite and indefinite articles, words made sense only through their disposition within a context. Incidentally, this is not too distant from the way neural networks operate: artificial intelligence enacts a regime of sense-making where identity is nothing but a stabilized pattern of differences in a mathematical field.

This is why Chinese thought departs from a preoccupation with the phenomenal world, or the world of the 'myriad things' (*wanwu* 万物), and the way these are positioned or organized. It attempts to decipher the propensity of things as they unfold and manifest themselves as forever changing phenomena in the one and only place, nurturing our response or resonance to them.

Where Parmenides inaugurates Western philosophy's search for an ontological ground for the existence of phenomena,

Chinese thought would rather see all things as temporary emergences within a relational whole. Things materialize in a given context, have their meaning defined in relation to the other things that surround them and eventually wither away and transform. More directly, things are not anything that exists with any level of autonomy but are, rather, the outcome of a *procedure*, of a way of cutting out or organizing, ultimately of a protocol.

In this sense, things function like events. Or rather, they *are* events. And their temporary or rather temporal nature means not simply that they have a beginning and an end – that they *are* in their *essence* within a given time – but instead, and more profoundly, that things *are* time. Time is not an external category in relation to which things would somehow be situated; it is not a transcendental condition or a prosthetic of access to them; temporality is given substance by the emergence of things and is equivalent to and wholly contained in that emergence, and that is the actual meaning of time.[14]

Likewise, things are not actually related *to* a context; they *are* the context. That whole within which things transform, just as the world that all together they form, is not any one thing deemed to be ontologically superior to the others, a universe understood as a container or a sum of things. It is, rather, a non-totalizable infinity of non-distinction or undefinition that cannot be grasped as a whole and transformed into an ontologically primary object. There is no spooky primordial soup of energy flows grounding everything else. It is, rather, the very emergence of certain phenomena that individuates specific things and thereby *produces the meaning of space* by defining an interiority and an exteriority, a boundary that only makes sense as a cut between the thing that has emerged and everything else.[15]

This is why, where Nietzsche wrestles with the limitations of metaphysical language, Chinese philosophy *wiggles* out of it by speaking the tongue of allusiveness. This very obliqueness is what triggers accusations of vagueness and incoherency from Western metaphysics, charges of poetry and mysticism.[16] Allusiveness, however, is not indicative of a *partial* access to the thing-in-itself: we approximate it, we come close to it, but, like an empathic Medusa, we never look at it in the eyes for fear of freezing it in stone. Allusion, rather, is what is left once we eliminate the *essential* nature of the object of reference, renouncing its individuality.[17] Allusion is not a heuristic vehicle of approximation to the real, but a pedagogical or soteriological tool helping to clear our presuppositions and dislocate our standpoint. Allusion does not serve to refer indirectly to that which cannot be grasped directly, it is not a strategy helping us tiptoe unseen toward the nudity of the thing-in-itself; rather, it is a negative allusion, or what remains of speech the moment it relinquishes all voyeuristic desire to spy on Being and to fall in love with its otherworldly beauty.

Truth is a betrayal

The philosopher, at least in the way that China has traditionally conceptualized such a figure, is not the individual who is able to grasp the real, the immutable or the true from within the flow of potentiality. The philosopher, on the contrary, is the person who can *keep open* that incessant flow without, unaware, falling in love with a single belief, object or perception, mistaking it for an eternal and solid certainty as opposed to a temporal and solidified event. Philosophers learn how to *respond* to things in their emergence; they focus their efforts not on climbing vertically but on nurturing their capacity to resonate with the event horizontally, in the same and only place they share. They do not *block* or *fix* whatever they encounter by discerning between what ultimately is and what ultimately is not, what belongs merely here and what belongs to the starry heavens.

In his principal work of metaphysics, *Correcting Youthful Ignorance* (正蒙, *Zheng Meng*), eleventh-century Song Confucian philosopher and politician Zhang Zai (张载, 1020–77) cautions precisely against partisan love: 'The sage embraces the myriad things and leaves nothing out. He can love the myriad things without partiality for any one of them.'[18] A maxim by Confucius encapsulates the same idea: 'Exemplary persons (*junzi*) are inclusive and not partisan; petty persons are partisan and not inclusive.'[19] This 'letting the world be' is equally captured in the Daoist *wu*-forms: *wuwei* 无为 *wuyu* 无欲 *wuzhi* 无知: noncoercive acting, objectless desiring and unprincipled or unmediated knowing. And in fact, in the *Daodejing* we find the same concept: 'Sages have no *fixed* heart-and-mind of their own.'[20] The principled person does not take up a definite position on anything, while the unprincipled clings to their belief as the only true and valid position.

Paradoxically, to be principled is to be without principles.

Take the story of Zhao Wen as found in the *Zhuangzi*, one of the key texts of Daoism.[21] Zhao was one of the most extraordinary lute players of China – with one caveat: he never played a single note. Zhao's hands could capture every harmony imaginable. He could, potentially, play any musical score and concoct the most celestial sounds. And yet, transforming that potentiality into an actuality – *actually* playing – would have implied choosing *one* note, one harmony, one scale from among the infinite possibilities offered to his fingers. How could he make such a choice? How could he betray the infinite? And so it is that Zhao decides to remain silent. Silence guards the unexpressed possibility of all harmony and all conceivable sound. Silence respects the infinity of all that can be; it lets it flow and keeps it vibrating with potentiality. On the other hand, letting one harmony *emerge* and favouring it, with enamoured eyes, over all the others, would *realize* and hence foreclose that potential. A similar predisposition can be found in the anecdote, recounted in the *Book of Jin*, concerning the life of Tao Yuanming, a famous poet who played a lute without any strings – a silent instrument.

A great player refrains from actually playing. Celebrated fourth-century Daoist philosopher Guo Xiang offers the following analysis of the story of Zhao Wen: 'The purpose of playing woodwinds and strings is to perform music. When some music is performed, other music is left out, but when no music at all is performed, [the whole body of all potential] music is left whole.'[22]

Confucius himself reminds us of Zhao Wen as he repeatedly claims he would rather remain silent: 'The Master said, "I think I will leave off speaking." "If you do not speak," Zigong replied, "how will we your followers find the proper way?" The Master responded, "Does *tian* 天 [the world] speak? And yet the four seasons turn and the myriad things are born and grow within it."'[23]

Speech *individuates* and *discriminates*. It elects and leaves out.

Just like the practice of allusion, such an attitude is in no way reducible to the European celebration of silence as the privileged route towards a secret essence inaccessible through language. This is not Heidegger's withdrawing Being that only poetry can approximate. It is neither Wittgenstein's quasi-religious 'Whereof one cannot speak', nor Bataille's mystical inner experience that words cannot express. For there is no *that* which we cannot speak about. There is no residue of the absolute or absolute residue timidly existing in secret. There is no Being and no approximation to or mourning for a lost Being and no secrecy beyond what is for all to see in the *monotopia* or the one and only place.

As philosopher and sinologist François Jullien has argued, we must draw a distinction between the Western concept of *impartiality*, normally understood as a fairness of judgement towards two opposing camps or propositions, and the classical Chinese conception of *non-partiality*, to be understood in the sense of globality, or the leaving-open of alternative possibilities and the refusal to definitely subscribe to one side and to pick a truth, an essence, a that-which-*is*. Jullien captures this with a powerful image: 'Every idea that's advanced closes at the very moment it opens; more precisely, it begins to foreclose other possible points of view in order to open the way for its own: there seems to be a necessary and yet arbitrary blindness at the beginning of all philosophizing . . . a philosopher will always begin by plucking out their eyes.'[24]

Plucking out their eyes. Blindness. These are unexpected words to identify a philosopher searching after truth. Philosophy, on the contrary, is defined by the eyes wide open of the individual who stands up in Plato's cave. Let there be light where shadows reigned. But classical Chinese thought seems to tell us the opposite: the origin of any utterance is darkness. To make a distinction – to solidify or privilege something over something else, one word over another, one action over the next – we must pluck out our eyes and numb our senses. The *Zhuangzi* uses this very same metaphor: 'Thus, it is said: "He who discriminates between alternatives fails to see clearly."'[25]

This is not the oracular blindness of the Greek prophet Tiresias, whose tortured eyes allowed him all the better to see the truth and pierce the veil of appearance. This is, rather, the blindness of the lover who murmurs 'I have eyes only for you'. We must betray all else that can be, abandon the incessant flow of potentiality, and become the lover of one.

Truth is a betrayal. Not merely the betrayal of one for another, as conceived in traditional sentimental parlance, but much more seriously the betrayal of the infinite for the one.

Philosophy, we know, is quite literally the love of knowledge. There is erotic ecstasy in the search after truth, as Plato so beautifully sings in the *Phaedrus*. Eros guides us to the One. And yet the Chinese predisposition is to merge the loving subject and the loved object. It is not love *for* knowledge that drives our attempt to capture ultimate, eternal truths; it is not the immutable forms that Eros the mediator lifts us up to. Rather, such truths and forms are indistinguishable from love – they *are* love. Truth emerges out of the partiality of judgement of a lover who has eyes for none other than their object of desire.

And so, if every utterance is but blind love, remaining silent is the choice of wisdom. Chastity instead of Platonic coitus. Holding back becomes the attitude of the virtuous person.

The virtuous person or the madman?

Creatio ex omnibus

Humans are bound to make choices. Confucian sages counsel rulers on the propitious course of actions; Daoist cooks master the art of slaughtering ox. The very meaning of being alive, of thinking, writing, playing or acting, is to privilege something over something else. We are not Zhao Wen. More fundamentally still, the world of things, animals and plants is not Zhao Wen: reality communicates and creates, and it does so all the time. The myriad things do not linger in a pure heaven of potentiality, but emerge in thunder and roar their presence. Breaking Zhao's silence is not a mere human affair: it is how the world constitutes an inside and an outside, how it *forms*, continuously.

A genuine superintelligence, understood as an *unbound* intelligence, would be destined to silence. In much Chinese thought, the existence of an omniscient being is ruled out as a possibility precisely for this reason: there is nothing that is complete, for being is premised on incompletion. To the extent that any intelligence speaks, it does so from a lack, a limitation, a deficit, a partiality, a malfunction even, upon which a temporary closure is grounded. Even artificial intelligence only runs on an engine of limitation. It is constrained by a limited initial dataset operating with a particular system architecture, and it is triggered by a specific prompt or intentionality that is regulated by a protocol.

In the absence of an objective or essential anchoring essence, speech, actions and the very meaning of *thing* all emerge by placing a stop and defining a sufficient context or situation to act. Truth, whether understood as the arrival point of a sequence of reasoning or the optimal result yielding a deliberation to act, is premised on a literal pulling of the plug, a desire to halt the search and to *settle*, a falling in love and in place. To break the silence – and hence to live – requires placing a stop to possibility. In the absence of a limit there would be no *thing*, but everything.

In Epicurean atomism, all things consist of indivisible atoms moving through the void. If these atoms moved in strictly parallel, vertical lines – as inherited from Democritean physics – then they would never interact, and no world could arise. To account for the emergence of order from chaos, Epicurus posits the *clinamen*, or swerve: a minute, spontaneous deviation in the motion of atoms. This swerve, though infinitesimal, introduces contingency into a system otherwise governed by necessity. The *clinamen* disrupts determinism allowing for the formation of compound bodies. It becomes a symbol of existential openness, a minimal tilt that makes possible both the cosmos and human autonomy. In a universe of falling atoms, it is this deviation, this act without cause, that opens the space for novelty, spontaneity and ethical responsibility. In our world, where, as we will continue to argue, no singular thing exists as such, the *clinamen* or the principle of genesis turns into its opposite: not a sudden interruption of order, but the creation of order and stability as a radically ungrounded gesture that can only be based on a deficiency and a limitation.

Limits are factual contingencies. They may be physical, intellectual, temporal and of a myriad other kinds. Had I indefinitely continued my reasoning, the word choice and the *settlement* reached – ultimately my *truth* or love – would have been different, but I may well have been dead by then, extinguished in madness or hunger. This is the sad fate of Buridan's donkey, which starved to death because it could not choose between two equidistant buckets of food. In slow systems such as human beings, or generally biological processes, limits are always at hand and only so much transformation would have been possible had I continued reflecting until factual contingencies placed a stop to my deliberation. Yet if one imagines an artificial intelligence of extreme speed, if one takes seriously quantum computing experiments that show a task that would have required years performed in seconds, and if one removes the human prompter with their biological limitation and imagines an autonomously desiring machine, then between thinking for three seconds or for five there could lie an abyss – and that means kinds of truths or choices separated by an abyss.

And so, one may legitimately ask, does *truth* depend on how much time I have before going hungry or before a computer runs out of energy? In a sense, yes. But rather than seeing finitude and closure as the other side of Being, the weak part that misses something, we may consider the budding closure of partiality as an act of *creativity* in a context where the lack of preference means nothing other than death by infinity.

Far from condemning all action as an illusion – because action implies choice, a favourite note that betrays all else – creativity plays a key role in Chinese thinking: 'In Daoism, it is captured in the dynamic and radically situated notions of non-coercive and spontaneous action (*wuwei* 无为), wandering at ease (*xiaoyaoyou* 逍遥游), and spontaneous arising (*ziran* 自然). Zhuangzi appeals to creative process in his claim that "the way is forged in the walking; things and events become so in the saying". Confucius, in the social context, makes this same point about human creativity in his claim that "it is persons who are able to extend the way, not the way that extends persons" . . . Even if there is no such thing as "Being", a myriad things are *brought into being*.'[26]

Creativity is then agential but not anthropocentric. It is a process, but it does not stem from a relation of cause and effect constituted by a moving subject and a moved object. It is, rather, creativity in the sense that a river 'rivers' its way to the sea, where matter itself does things with matter the way perlocutionary speech does things with words. All that *is* can only *be* to the extent that it shows creativity, that it's there, that it obtains – and only for as long as it *remains* or *stays* or for as long as its verbal form applies: the river is a river for as long as it *rivers*. Creativity is the summon or solidification of a thing, its acquisition of a transitory state of presence, of having, of obtaining, its emerging out of indistinction. It is the *realization* of the event.

This type of creativity is opposed as much to Greek philosophies of Being as it is to Judeo-Christian theology of creation from nothing. In a polemic against individualism, John Gray points out that the idea of creation originates in Jewish religion: 'In ancient Greek thinking, the world is everlasting. Plato's Forms are out of time; the visible world is a cave of flickering shadows. In the Hebrew bible, the world and the soul are created by God from nothingness. The modern ideal of self-creation, which has reached its self-destroying apotheosis in the liberal West, is forgotten theology filtered through a Romantic cult of personality.'[27] But where creation out of nothingness, or the transformation of *nothing* into *something*, contains the heroic claim to originality of the modern mind facing the absence of Being, flirting with Chinese inclinations allows us to discover a different concept of creativity: a process of transformation of *everything* into *something*, or the individuation of potentiality as a humble act of simplification without end.

Creatio ex omnibus instead of *creatio ex nihilo*.

Martin Heidegger writes: 'Remaining, stopping means: to endure, to stand firm, to come to a halt and to dwell in itself, thus to remain at rest. Goethe says in a beautiful line:

"Die Fiedel stockt, der Tänzer weilt" (The violin falls silent, the dancer stops). But to halt, to remain, to endure and to persist is the ancient meaning of the word "to be".'[28] The ontological creativity represented by Zhao Wen's lute is exactly the opposite of this. For the musician to halt and to endure is inseparable from playing and creating. Letting things be, *realizing* them, means to sequester them from the indistinct potentiality of everything and to let them emerge and stay for as long as they continue reverberating with that creativity. The violin sings, the dancer jumps. This is the meaning of the word 'to be'.

Where befits the moment

In China's eventful world, form that cannot be separated from temporality becomes cadence or rhythm, and the aestheticization of experience becomes a musicality. The philosopher does not search for the true object hiding behind the shades of myriad things, but for the metric of their disposition and the harmony of their incessant transformation.

There is no historical disclosure of Being that allows beings to enter into play and truth conditions to emerge. It is the immanent organization of particulars and their ever shifting disposition that form and inform meaning. While Heidegger's hero catapults the world onto a new disclosure of Being, majestically reorienting what can count as real, true or meaningful, the principle of horizontal mediation replaces the gesture of momentous transformation with a steady but humble housekeeping, a work of continuous, creative and concrete reorganization of the cartography of particulars.

The philosopher, and indeed any creature and any thing, *mediates* to the extent they contribute to reorganizing the disposition of the myriad things – to changing their *protocol*, the way they operate.

Etymologically, mediation is the act of being-in-the-middle or standing between two sides to connect or reconcile them. But the classical Chinese concept of the *mean* is to be understood as neither the middle-*point* between two opposites, nor, with Aristotle, as a sense of moderation between extremes.[29] Both a mathematical middle and a mean as a *logos* of moderation would refer to a specific *point*, and hence a solidified position. The Chinese mean is rather dynamic, or, better, *a* dynamic, a principle of dynamism, not a static position but an energy. It points to the ability to shift or flow along the infinite spectrum of possibility, remaining open to multiple potentials and to changing one's positions. The mean is an elusive and ever shifting point that serves to scratch the glue that plasters us to a singular position for too long.

But where ought the mean to lie if one should ever settle? What note should one play if we are to create music? If we accept that we speak and act, that we let choices emerge, that things are formed, then what guides and organizes such creativity? How ought we to dispose the particulars at hand?

Confucianism has a text entirely dedicated to this question: the Zhongyong 中庸, traditionally attributed to Zisi 子思.[30] Often translated as *The Doctrine of the Mean*, the text represents a guide to harmonious action. Roger Ames and David Hall choose to render the title as *Focusing the Familiar*, wishing to underline the nature of the *mean* (*Zhong* 中) as the dynamic realization of the focus and equilibrium of the whole, as well as the familiarity or ordinariness of the world that one wishes to put in focus.

The very opening section of the *Zhongyong* sets the task as one of *harmonizing* that which emerges to ensure that all things may flourish: 'The moment at which joy and anger, grief and pleasure, have yet to arise is called a nascent equilibrium (*zhong* 中); once the emotions have arisen, that they are all brought into proper focus (*zhong*) is called harmony (*he* 和). This notion of equilibrium and focus (*zhong*) is the great root of the world; harmony then is the advancing of the proper way in the world. When equilibrium and focus are sustained and harmony is fully realized, the heavens and earth maintain their proper places and all things flourish in the world.'[31]

The process of *focusing* takes place against a plane of immediacy. It is a mediation that sits alongside the mediated. The character *yong* 庸 of *Zhongyong* 中庸 can be read as referring to something that 'continues to be utilized' and hence becomes a 'habit', and in this sense it is something 'ordinary', even 'banal', and which exists 'everywhere'[32] (in the one and only place). This making-habitual, or the creation of a *habit* as a disposition, can be understood as an embodied limitation of the possible. Just as in traditional ontology defining what 'is not' allows what 'is' to emerge, separating it from the plane of indistinction, so focusing the *mean* of a situation is really an operation of optical focus, or an ontology of creation, an *ontopoiesis* that realizes the contours of a particular action or thing and lets it come into focus.

Ultimately, equilibrium or the mean lies where *befits the moment*; it is the position that is productive of harmony within the present state of the world. Where most European philosophy attempted a transcendence of the merely-at-hand, escaping the finite ends of ordinary human practice by fixating the philosopher's gaze on the starry sky of Being, on a *logos* that orders the totality, or again in the mind of a Subject, the Chinese predisposition is, rather, to ennoble an engagement with the finite not by ontologically surpassing it, but by harmonizing it, by organizing the plurality of finites and their relationality in a way that is productive, or *formative*, of harmony within the *monotopia*.

Harmony, too, becomes a verb: *to harmonize*. And as contemporary Chinese philosopher Xiang Shuchen underlines, harmony so understood is a creative process: 'The capacity to see how a situation can become harmonized requires both an intimate knowledge of the nature of the particulars and an imagination creative enough to reconcile all these particulars into a coherent and resonant network of relationships.'[33]

Chinese thought presents a symbiotic relationship between the way the world inclines and human experience that is based neither on absolute principles nor on mere caprice. Rather, life is guided by the search for what best *resonates* (*gǎnyìng* 感应 or *gǎntōng* 感通)[34] with a particular state of the world. Letting things emerge in this way – *creating*[35] things in this way, and not remaining silent – is an empirical rather than a metaphysical process, an ordinary practice that isolates not an ultimate truth but, rather, a contingent use-value. The way one harmonizes is by looking for resonance: the path of least opposition, the way the disposition of the particulars at hand inclines itself. And if something resonates with a specific moment, then it follows that not all things are at all times equal, and not any choice is a mere whim or theatre of the absurd.

If nothing is forever true and better because there is no universal law that grounds a permanent distinction; if, deeper still, nothing really and forever *is* because all formations are always temporary and dependent – then still, some things really are better than others at specific times and under specific conditions, and they *are* so in the fullest and only sense of the word. Being is nothing but being-in-position, being-in-context and being-in-relation, and this is not the weak side of anything else standing above or beyond it, but the one and only way of being in the one and only place.

Just as the Confucian *Zhongyong* tries to elucidate the process through which harmony is established, so the *Huainanzi* 淮南子 is at once a Daoist compendium of knowledge and a manual for governance and self-cultivation, explaining how enlightened individuals can attune themselves to the world to achieve harmony and act in accordance with the natural flow of the universe. It is no coincidence that Confucian or Daoist texts, missing the possibility of clearly pointing to *that which is* (which is right, true, appropriate, virtuous), convey indications for self-cultivation. This is a modal and situated ethics, in the sense of developing a habitude or disposition concerning how to act across differing situations as the specificities of conduct resist generalization. There is no question of discovering a stable order of things that is always already given; rather, the Way is synonymous with a creative process that *orders* the particulars and *gives* them a way.

The wise person is whoever agrees with the resonance; that is to say, whoever learns the secrets of alignment, constructing oneself in such a way as to constantly tune one's own internal inclination with the discontinuous transformations of the world.

But how is the world, truly?

And yet, don't we have here a return of the penchant for fixity and for grasping the order of a totality?

In his lecture notes on the philosophy of Nietzsche, Reiner Schürmann presents the following interpretation of one of the most famous fragments from Heraclitus ('Listening not to me but to the Logos it is wise to agree that all things are one').[36] Schürmann comments: 'I retain from this only the verb translated by "to agree" = *homologein*. The wise is the one who homologizes, i.e. conforms the logos in him to the logos of all things.' He continues: 'Heraclitus has another expression for such espousal of the discontinuous: "Wisdom is to say the true and to act according to the nature of things [*poiein kata physin*], listening to them" (fragment 112, trans. Bruno Snell). If one takes the word *physis* literally, it does not mean "nature", but – from the verb *phyesthai* – "to grow, to come about"; just as *nasci*. Wisdom, then, is to act ("poiein" in the pre-Aristotelian sense which encompasses *prattein*) in accordance with things as they come about.'[37]

The wise are those who homologize, conforming the *logos* in them to the *logos* of all things. Wisdom is to be continuously born in accordance with the way the world unfolds. Just as in the Chinese case, the objective is reaching a symbiosis between the unfolding of the world and human experience. And yet there is a singular way, a law, a principle: the *logos* above me that guides the *logos* inside me.

We should be able to say something apparently impossible: the world is continuous creation, and this very statement is a creation. Daoism, for instance, does say precisely this: '*Dao* 道 has been described as an emerging pattern of relatedness as perceived from the perspective of a given particular, or *de* 德. The perceived order is an achievement, not a given. Because *dao* is an emergent, "bottom-up" order rather than something imposed.'[38]

But aren't we then returned to Aristotle's paradox of relativism? If the world *is* in any particular way, including in the way of having no way, then we are contradicting ourselves in arguing that there is no particular structure of the world. If the world both *is* and *is not* the way we say *it is*, then we plunge into meaninglessness and into the mutism of a plant.

Classical Chinese philosophy escapes this predicament by indirectly highlighting a crucial disposition or inclination: discarding ultimate truths does not result in mere silence or a suspension of life *because this would once again solidify belief into a new place.* If we take the thought of becoming as a new *ground*, if we turn it into a *law* that governs the world and that we must adhere and be faithful to, then we would reify it, or turn it into a static thing, an essence that is superior, and hence not equal, to everything else – the way the world truly is. But if we did this, then we would have created another top–down universal, a stiffening of our predisposition, a blockage in the dynamism of the *mean* and the search for that which befits the moment.

This is how we wiggle out of the threat of Aristotle's rebuttal of relativism. Why, in fact, should the belief that all things are indifferently equal be considered any truer – any less susceptible to being just one emergence from the flow of infinite possibility – than claiming preference for one thing over the other? The equality of all things is the dynamic that allows preference to emerge. Byung-Chul Han brings this out in discussing the position of *love* in the Zhuangzi: 'Both love and friendship presuppose distinction and partiality, as they are founded on desire. Thus, the sage does not "love" the human being, nor cultivates any "friendship". Love is something non-existent, and friendship produces bonds. Yet the sage is not entirely detached: detachment would again presuppose a well-defined subject of interest, indifferent to the world.'[39]

The opposition between the plane of indistinction or potentiality and the emergence or realization of a choice – the opposition between Zhao Wen's silence and the mundane mandolin player – is a false opposition: all is but creativity. Zhao Wen's silence, his refusal to play any note not to betray the infinity of possibility is to be understood, quite literally, as a gesture, an allusion, and not a statement of knowledge; there is no higher reality hidden behind the cacophony of musical play, there is no Divine Silence providing a higher ground on which to stand and from which to look down with condensation on the amateur players. The gesture towards silence performs a heuristic or soteriological function: emptying out all distinctions from the arrogance of existing in a way that is truer than anything else, bringing back onto the same horizontal plane the distinct and the indistinct, the everyday action and the deepest mystical thought seen to ground it.

Just like John Cage's *4′33″*, which performs a silence, we pass through Zhao's aphonia to return to the necessity of word and music, including the word and music that silence inescapably represents, and hence to a liberated approach towards creativity. The gesturing, the allusion, the mysticism even of much

Eastern thought all lie exactly here: it is a physical push that dislocates our body and enables us not to keep silent like a plant, but to speak wisely; not to remain unmoved, but to love maturely.

मध्यमाप्रतपिदा

Indian philosophy occupies a geo-philosophically precious location between Europe and China. It has a grammatical concept of Being, sharing linguistic and hence conceptual roots with Europe, but it has spent more energy than any in turning that essentialist departure point against itself, crafting an ontology of ontological overcoming. In this sense, India really hosts the thought of the Middle between East and West.

Far from a simple existential manual or guide through the rhythmic cadence of life, the reduction of Being to being-there challenges some of the key assumptions of ontology. If in Chinese philosophy this challenge is mostly implicit, for lack of an essentialist ontology to debunk in the first place, its philosophical radicality comes out explicitly in several currents of Indian thought.

We will delve deeper into the concept of ontological creativity, or *ontopoiesis*, discussing philosopher and monk Nāgārjuna, active in the second century CE and founder of the Mādhyamika school of Buddhism. A similar disposition, however, can equally be found in Hinduism, for instance in the *Brihadaranyaka Upanishad* or in the tradition of Vedanta.[40] Nāgārjuna's central work, *The Fundamental Wisdom of the Middle Way*, introduces the idea of a Twofold Truth composed of a conventional truth (*samvrtisatya*), applying to the phenomenal world, and one supreme truth (*paramārthasatya*), applying to the realization of the nothingness or emptiness of the phenomenal world. Conventional and ultimate truths are not presented, as in Greek thought, as one truth and one opinion, *aletheia* and *doxa*, or one essence and one appearance, but genuinely as *two truths* that are of equivalent value.[41] Being equals becoming; that which inherently *is* equals that which inherently *is not*. The following passage is where such equivalence is drawn out, giving us a chance to present some of the main tenets of Nāgārjuna's thought:

> Whatever is dependently co-arisen
> That is explained to be emptiness
> That, being a dependent designation,
> Is itself the Middle Way. (24:18)

The first line of the stanza speaks of co-dependent origination. This is the Buddhist principle of *pratītyasamutpāda*, describing the interdependency of things: nothing exists in isolation, but all is in relation. Japanese Kyoto School philosopher Yamauchi Tokuryū, who dedicated a long study to the relation between Nāgārjuna's thought and Greek philosophy, translates this as *co-attendance*, or '*sodai*' (相待) in Japanese. Another possible translation points towards the logic of *co-becoming*, referred to as '*gongsheng*' (共生) in Chinese and '*kyōsei*' (共生) in Japanese and gesturing to 'symbiosis', 'coexistence' or 'living together'.[42] Both translations emphasize that entities develop and evolve together through mutual interactions, so that phenomena do not exist independently but are fundamentally the product of a connection.

That co-dependent things are 'empty' – this is the second line of the stanza – means that they are deprived of a strong identity as they only exist relationally and hence not in-themselves. Things are exactly the opposite of what René Descartes calls a *substance* in his *Principles of Philosophy*, namely 'a thing which so exists that it needs no other thing in order to exist' (I, §51). Critiquing and radicalizing the canonical interpretation of the *Abhidharma* – the third-century BCE classical compendium of Buddhist teachings and commentaries – Nāgārjuna takes aim at the concept of *svabhāva*, or the idea of things existing intrinsically (atomically), even as they originally emerge co-dependently. Co-arisen phenomena are defined by their lack of *ipseity* or individual identity. Things, outside conventions and outside their temporary relational position to other things (their place in the cartography of particulars), do not exist; they *are* not in any inherent sense, they are *empty*. Tokuryū argues that in European philosophy things 'possess their autonomy, a strong ego or at least their identity, and in this are solid. The self is the self, the other is the other'; on the other hand, co-dependent things 'co-become with one another, or at least flirt with one another, and as a result will have a weak self-identity, or at least a weak ego'.[43] If things only exist in relation, then nothing ultimately *is* but only temporarily *remains* (in position).[44]

The third line of the stanza serves to bring out the idea that to see *both* things *and* emptiness in this way is to conceive of them in their mundane existence, or in worldly convention. *Both* the world of phenomena *and* emptiness, both conventional and supreme truths, are themselves co-dependent or empty: one does not exist more fundamentally than the other.

Finally, precisely this mundane, co-dependent existence of both the world of phenomena and the ultimate reality of emptiness – concludes the fourth line of the stanza – is the meaning of the Middle Way. The Middle Way points to the equivalence of all reality, as both mundane and ultimate truths both occupy the same and only place, or the *monotopia*.

With this in mind, let us see how Nāgārjuna turns the logic of Being on its head and hence returns us to the primacy of creativity.

The tetralemma

Inheriting the inclination of Parmenides and Zeno, the main tradition of European philosophy presents us with a *bivalent* thought, nurtured to distinguish between Being and becoming, affirmation and negation. Being literally extracts difference from the uniformity of non-Being: it is the European principle of emergence, whereby things *are* and hence they become individuated and separated from indistinction by reference to what they *are not*. The world comes alive through Being – it appears composed of trees and apples, dogs and cats, love and hate, and not of a uniform, indistinguishable continuum of experience. The principle of non-contradiction is the route that Aristotle sculpts in the European mind to avoid collapsing all things into an undifferentiated One – refuting it would mean accepting that a man is also a horse and also a tree.[45]

Contemporary Chinese philosopher Zhao Tingyang describes this as a type of 'dictionary thinking'[46] that is categorical in setting boundaries or definitions on things, and is ultimately descriptive in being limited by a given reality that is considered to have its own, independent objecthood. Knowledge of Being *fixes* – it chooses while relinquishing all agency, it grounds the playing of a particular note while claiming its inevitability; in this sense, as Nietzsche so well understood, it is a principle of sanity or, as Zhao Tingyang puts it, of economy, albeit one that hides its merely therapeutic nature – a medicine, as Buddha says to Kasyapa, that won't speak its name and won't leave the body.

Nāgārjuna instead liberates things from the straitjacket of identity. His Middle Way is ultimately the reversal of the principle of the excluded middle, denying that any one thing must either 'be' or 'not be'. Such reversal transforms the European *di*lemma – to be or not to be[47] – in a *tetra*lemma, disrupting Hamlet's despair by offering a field of four creative options in lieu of a stark affirmation or negation. Nāgārjuna's *tetralemma* adds to the Western binary logic two other propositions: that something *neither is nor is not*, hence negating both affirmation and negation, and that something *both is and is not*, affirming both the affirmation and the negation.

Let us see this at play. In a key passage of *The Fundamental Wisdom of the Middle Way*, Nāgārjuna presents us with an accusation of nihilism levied at his own philosophy by an imaginary opponent. This accusation will be shown to derive from a dualistic or bivalent understanding of the relation of Being and not-being and to wither away with it. His opponent says:

> If all of this is empty,
> Neither arising, nor ceasing,
> Then for you, it follows that
> The Four Noble Truths do not exist. (24:1)

In this stanza and those that follow, the fictional critic is arguing that if Nāgārjuna establishes emptiness or non-being as the ultimate truth of his philosophy, then it follows that nothing *is*, and hence no truths exist, and hence nothing remains and all is debased and devalued. Answering this challenge is what will allow Nāgārjuna to clarify his concept of emptiness or nothingness. Nāgārjuna had already gestured to a way out:

> To say 'it is' is to grasp for permanence.
> To say 'it is not' is to adopt the view of nihilism.
> Therefore a wise person
> Does not say 'exists' or 'does not exist'. (15:10)

Here, Nāgārjuna paraphrases the *Discourse to Katyāyana*, where Buddha advocates for a path that avoids the extremes of essentialism and nihilism, advancing instead the middle path of acknowledging phenomena without attributing to them inherent existence. Nāgārjuna gives philosophical substance to this intuition by elucidating that middle path lying between 'it is' and 'it is not'.

For Nāgārjuna, the Middle is nothingness, emptiness, void. But if it is a mistake to see Being as existing substantially, a-temporally, outside contingence, it is also a mistake to simply affirm emptiness as an absolute *nihil* that is something and has an essence. If we hold on to emptiness as if it were a real, substantial truth, then it can destroy us 'like a snake wrongly grasped' (Nāgārjuna 24.11). Emptiness is not separated from and superior to the phenomenal world, inhabiting another place. Emptiness is not starkly in opposition to Being, existing essentially as its negation, as the other pole of a dichotomous dilemma; rather, it unfolds in the very world of phenomena and represents the comprehension of the non-substantiality of things in their mundane nature. There is no emptiness that is not the emptiness of entities, emptiness as new awareness of, and in relation to, the phenomenal world.

> Were there a trace of something
> There would be a trace of emptiness
> Were there no trace of anything
> There would be no trace of emptiness. (13:7)

The emptiness that Nāgārjuna describes is predicated *of* something but is not in itself anything, and that predication, just as we saw in the case of harmony, takes the form of a verb rather than a noun – *emptying out* rather than *the empty*. Nothingness is a constant process of becoming-void, a voiding of phenomenal things as much as a 'voiding the void',[48] a negation that negates the negation itself. As Tokuryū poetically puts it, 'the negation discussed in the *Treaty of the Middle* burns all things, to the point of burning the burning itself'.[49] In short, emptiness, or rather emptying, is itself an act of creativity, not a noun but a verb and an action.

This can be understood as a 'negation without negator' – for if there was a negator there would be a subject, a *thing* standing behind the negation ('the empty'). Nāgārjuna highlighted the unity of subject and predicate in the maxim *gantā na gacchati*, 'the goer does not go': for just as there is no *goer* that can exist separately from the act of *going*, so there is no *emptiness which empties*, existing independently of the act; or, in fact, there is no emptiness at all, but only the verbal emptying-out, including of emptiness itself.

One must refuse to objectify, make-substance, make-Being, ultimately refuse to fall in love, including, as Byung-Chul Han warned, with the idea of lovelessness itself. This is the key significance of negating not only the affirmation but, equally, the negation, or the third proposition of the tetralemma: 'not', the empty, *is not – it neither is nor is not.*

So much convolution to remove the thought of Being and immunize the mind from Parmenides! And yet, it is from this double negation that advances a *double affirmation*, enshrined by the fourth preposition of the tetralemma.

Let us go back to the challenge of nihilism: if all is seen to be empty then nothing truly exists, argued the opponent. We can see now that this critique only works within the dilemmic logic of Being. For it is in that dilemma that we can either claim that things are as they appear, that things exist as we perceive them, that the shadows on the walls 'are' and they are not 'not', not empty, or, swapping the pole that we choose to objectify, argue instead that only the absolute really exists, and if we believe that the ultimate reality is emptiness then only emptiness is essential and real, and hence all phenomena of the world are devalued and seen to inhabit a lesser place. Both choices presuppose that to exist with value is to exist inherently, essentially; they only differ in whether the inherent existence, the in-itself, is attributed to phenomena or to an ultimate nature, form or absolute, including an absolute nothingness, standing guard behind them.

The two poles, Nāgārjuna can now tell us, are not at all in dichotomous opposition but are, rather, at one with each other. The double negation of essence is not a *lack*, a diminishment or *mere* appearance. The Middle Way, as the emptying of all things and the emptying of emptiness itself, is the principle that informs the overcoming of the dichotomy and that supports the fourth principle of the tetralemma, the thought that things *both are and are not*. The double affirmation – really, a return to the world, an affirmation of the world in the sense Nietzsche intuited in his happiest moments – underlines that it is precisely because things are empty that they can co-dependently arise. It is the very lack of static self-identity, the lack of *ipseity*, of egos, that enables things to co-become and hence to be in the first place. It is because things *are not* that they can be.

And so, we can let them be. We can nurture them and transform them and treat them without condescendence or elevation, but as companions in the play of creativity and *ontopoiesis*.

So all is transformation?

Again: such an ethos of creation, such predisposition to becoming – isn't it all yet another point of view on the way the world *is*? And, if so, isn't that a return to a philosophy of the Being of the world? And if it isn't, would such a philosophy not have to accept its opposite, so that, if nothing can be said to inherently flow, then things may not flow at all and actually be stable?

Heraclitus presents us with a philosophy of transformation, as his Fragment B90 makes clear: 'All things are exchanged for fire and fire for all things, as goods for gold and gold for goods.'[50] As Tokuryū points out, Heraclitus has made fire the principle of the constitution of things because fire is a form of exchange. Fire indicates the insubstantiality and constant transformation of all. And yet, just as fire consumes things, something compensates for that consumption. Crucially, this flow of transformations happens according to an *order* – what is lost must be compensated, what empties must be filled. And this order follows the *laws* that govern nature, and these laws make the *logos* (the one we must 'listen to'). This is what makes Heraclitus lose the sceptre of philosopher of becoming to transform into a dogmatic or at least an essentialist thinker, ultimately a thinker of Being, for his becoming can never become the blockage of becoming but *must* always become, and that necessity represents the *logos* of the universe.

This is a most uncanny companion to much anti- or post-metaphysical philosophy. Nietzsche, for instance, may have done away with both the real and the apparent world,[51] but at least in a possible reading of his philosophy the world *must* dance, as cosmic becoming objectifies in a Will to Power that grounds the bubbling *stability* of that which becomes, its erupting *predictability* – for things bubble, they erupt, of necessity and inescapably.

Isn't Nāgārjuna doing the same, liquefying each and every thing except his own viewpoint on the co-becoming of all?

Interestingly, he gives great attention to the traditional reduction to absurdity of any allegedly relativist claim: if things are said to be ultimately non-existent, then this applies to this very thesis; hence, this thesis denies itself. Nāgārjuna even dedicates an entire treaty, the *Vigrahavyāvartanī*, precisely to refuting it, clearing the ground for a philosophical experiment that Greek thought blocked through the marginalization of the sophists and its anchorage to Being.[52] Nāgārjuna's way out is simple: the relativist objection only applies within the dichotomous thought that foresees the necessary existence of Being and that finds a problem with the idea that, if the thesis 'is', then, at the same time, it 'is not'. The dilemma is not solved but sidestepped and transformed into a tetralemma, where the opening of a space of double negation and double affirmation, or the revaluation of the phenomenal as monotopic, singular reality encompassing both the absolute and the everyday, dissolves and wiggles out of the critique. Nāgārjuna's thesis 'is' in the very same way that it claims that all other things 'are': it is and it is not, it neither and both is nor is not.

Nāgārjuna goes further. His deployment of the tetralemma is not meant to catalogue the possible modes of Being, but to dismantle the very presupposition that things must conform to any fixed ontological category. Startlingly, in multiple places Nāgārjuna shows that each of the four propositions of the tetralemma generates contradiction or incoherence once examined in the light of co-dependent origination – and goes as far as *negating the tetralemma*, and then negating the negation of the tetralemma, and so on. The point here is to cut off the reflex that language and thought must anchor phenomena in some determinate metaphysical status – making of Nāgārjuna's own system a new stable anchor, a ground, an originary *arché*. What remains through the negation of the four principles of the tetralemma is not a hidden fifth option, but the realization that the framework of ontological predication itself is misguided. Again, this is a heuristic or soteriological move preventing us from hypostatizing concepts into substances, and instead orienting thought towards the dynamic, interdependent play of creativity.

Consider, for instance, the distinction between the abstract knowledge of the role that nature plays in the world and the *feeling* of it. If I fully understand, say, Bruno Latour's actor network theory and consider all nonhuman things as agents capable of action, but I do so only logically, abstractly, as a principle and a set of ideas, but without *actually feeling a tree thus*, without feeling it as a fellow agent, do I fully understand Latour's theory? There is a complementary form of understanding: *actually* lingering on the tree, and doing so sufficiently at length and sufficiently often that the abstract knowledge of its agential role comes to be perceived *immediately*, without the mediation of concepts or theories, but simply as that which goes without saying, springing spontaneously from the tree. The purpose of much Chinese or Indian philosophy is to trigger such a state, aiding the emergence of an individual disposition that incarnates and hence accomplishes the ideas as actually operating vectors of existential creativity and transformation.

Nāgārjuna's tetralemma ultimately serves to incline us to the realization that emptiness, and hence enlightenment, cannot take place anywhere else but on the same plane as the phenomenal world. Being has a vertical relation to the beings that it allows to distinguish and make-emerge. It lies above or below, in front, behind or inside, but never in the same place. But the Middle Way is in-between, not above or below. This is the significance of the equivalence of *samsāra* and *nirvāna*, quite literally their collapsing into a *monotopia*, that Nāgārjuna brings out at the end of his book:

> There is not the slightest difference
> Between cyclic existence and nirvāna.
> There is not the slightest difference
> Between nirvāna and cyclic existence. (25:19)

It is no coincidence that precisely such equivalence, which returns us to the Chinese penchant for ordinary practice and immanent analysis, would be made the central precept of *Tiantai*, one of the key schools of Chinese Buddhism.[53] Here is an injunction to revalue things in their mundane existence, at once refusing to ascribe to them any existence-in-itself and refusing to search behind their back for some kind of elusive, otherworld absolute, including the absolute of this very injunction, *which you are free to negate* in an act of ontopoietic creativity.

Just like Kazimir Malevich's canvas *White on White*, which paints an absence, we pass through Nāgārjuna's emptiness to return to the fullness of brush and paint and hence to a liberated approach towards creativity. Here, again, is the physical push that dislocates our body and enables us not to keep silent like a plant but to speak wisely, not to remain unmoved but to love maturely.

The phenomenon

About five hundred years before Nāgārjuna analysed it, the tetralemma showed up in ancient Greece: 'Things are equally indifferent, unstable, and indeterminate; for this reason, neither our perceptions nor our beliefs tell the truth or lie. For this reason, then, we should not trust them, but should be without opinions, without inclinations, without wavering, *saying of every single thing that "it is no more this than is not, or both is and is not, or neither is nor is not"*.'[54]

This phrase is attributed to fourth-century BCE Pyrrho of Elis, possibly the first philosopher in world history to be exposed to both Greek and Indian sensibilities. Pyrrho followed Alexander the Great on his Asian campaigns, reaching the borders of present-day India. According to Plutarch, Alexander the Great met Indian ascetic philosophers – termed *gymnosophists*, literally 'naked wise men' – near the Indus River, and specifically in Taxila, in present-day Punjab, Pakistan. The gymnosophists encountered by the Greeks were most likely members of several different ascetic traditions, including Jain Digambaras, Ajivikas and possibly Buddhist or Brahmanical sannyasins.[55] Pyrrho, Plutarch confirms, was with Alexander the Great during the encounter. Among the ascetics was one man, called Kalanos by the Greeks, who would spend one year, or according to some accounts even two, together with Alexander's expedition.

Timon of Phlius, a student and follower of Pyrrho, notes that Pyrrhonian philosophy leads to the negation of both the principle of non-contradiction and the principle of the excluded middle as formulated by Aristotle. The irony, of course, is that Aristotle was none other than Alexander the Great's tutor. And it is his pupil's world-historical military expansion that would facilitate the refutation of his teacher's key metaphysical tenets by enabling contact with a very different philosophical tradition. Pyrrho, however, does more than merely reverse Aristotle's founding principles: the dilemma is transformed into a tetralemma, explicitly adding that things *both are and are not* and *neither are nor are not.* The significance of Nāgārjuna's tetralemma, as we have seen, is not merely to undo the dichotomy of contradiction, but to grow us out of the very distinction between Being and appearance that grounds it, allowing us to wiggle out of the contradiction of relativism and return to a new conception of ontological creativity.

Pyrrho has a similar objective.

Pyrrho is not merely a subjectivist, a traditional sceptic or a relativist, someone for whom 'all is appearance' *within the terms of the confrontation drawn by Parmenides,* whereby appearance is precisely non-Being, the weak side of reality, the fleeting and the changing defined as the opposite of the non-fleeting and the unchangeable. Pyrrho does not accept but transforms the rules of the game. Appearance, in his sense, becomes liberated and empowered. Appearances are neither appearances-*of* (something) nor appearances-*for* (someone). This would leave untouched, respectively, the idea of a unitary object or a unitary subject as the *real* transmitting or receiving end of the appearance, as its kernel or ground. But appearances do not occupy the other side of Being. Rather, they inhabit a singular and immanent place, the only place of reality, or a *monotopia.* The scandal and radicality represented by Pyrrho's thought in a Greek context lies entirely here: dislocating our comprehension of the world away from its division between *two places*: one real, one merely apparent.[56]

That radicality explains why Pyrrhonian thought would constantly be reduced to a tame *epistemic* scepticism towards what *can be said* to be really there, as opposed to an *ontological* scepticism aiming at the total dissolution of any distinction between the real and the apparent world. The taming of Pyrrhonian scepticism would cage the development of European thought around the dichotomy of Being and becoming, failing to grasp the possibility of its simple *withering away* as a place of dualistic opposition.

The true nihilism of European metaphysics lies not in refusing to believe in Being, but, on the contrary, in *refusing to see life outside an anchorage to Being*, in not seeing enough life or life real enough in an existence horizontally anchored to this one and only place. Pyrrho's repudiation of the separation between shadows and reality is largely a gesture that points to a possible way of living without such a dualistic break. He offers no *confutation* of Aristotle's principle of non-contradiction: Pyrrho accepts that whoever negates it negates Being, for, if anything can also be anything else, then nothing 'is'. But rather than seeing absurdity, Pyrrho sees liberated life, and, like Nāgārjuna, gestures to the possibility of a different inclination towards the consequences of contradiction.

The result of this Pyrrhonian inclination, says Timon, is first *aphasia* – literally, non-saying – and then *ataraxia* – tranquillity or the absence of disturbance. In Sextus Empiricus's *Outlines of Pyrrhonism*, aphasia is one of the key consequences of *epoché*, the suspension of judgement. In traditional *epistemic* scepticism, *epoché* refers to the refusal to affirm or deny any proposition about the nature of reality, given the impossibility of accessing reality itself. Pyrrho, however, takes this one step further – with the same manoeuvre we have discussed in the context of Confucianism, Daoism and Buddhism. The refusal to speak is not a sign of respect for Being's inaccessibility, nor a poetic approximation to the timidity of truth, but rather a vehicle to *undo the distinction* between Being and appearance, learning the art of speaking without solidity – that is, understanding speaking as solidifying temporarily, ultimately as *creating*, and not as the mediating access to a pre-existing stability. *Poieis* and not *logos*.

Sounding just like a Chinese sage, Pyrrho outlines his rule of personal conduct: 'To be without judgement, without inclining to any side.'[57] This is not a suspension of judgement in the traditional sceptical sense of an inability to judge things due to our *uncertainty* concerning their nature, but rather points to an *abstention* of judgement in the sense we have seen Zhao Wen giving to the practice: a refusal to objectify, to take an appearance as an appearance-of, as a pointer to another place that is fuller and truer, where all is order and beauty.

Aristotle tried to bring sceptics onto the prairie of self-contradiction by showing that their theoretical indifference to all things, the lack of distinction between opposites, is disproven by their very life at each moment they decide to eat instead of starving, of wearing a costume instead of freezing in the cold. And yet this critique unveils Aristotle's own particularistic blind spots: that one must have a reason to act, and that reason is understood only in relation to what essentially is. But there is no need for a ground to ground action. On the contrary, the dissolution of essence and of Being returns lightness to movement – not a solid, but a process of solidifying, always partial, but only to the extent that all is partiality, and hence the partial nature of a choice is no reason to discriminate its emergence and hold back.

One day, while walking, Pyrrho came upon a hole in the ground. His companions warned him of the risk. But, sticking to his principle of suspending judgement about all things, he refused to acknowledge the hole as real, walking straight ahead and willingly falling into the pit. Pyrrho, of course, did not live like this. Indeed, he lived to the rather exceptional age of ninety. The pantomime served, rather, as a pedagogical vehicle for the benefit of his pupils. The hole does not exist in-itself, and the act of falling into it is but a shocking way of conveying, of *showing*, freedom from Being. Just like Confucius' refusal to speak. With the caveat that, once freed, one *returns to the world* and avoids the hole (which *is* not, but *stays* there in a *context* where we would rather stay alive).

It is, then, no coincidence that Pyrrho's conception of nothingness undergoes the same transformation we have seen taking shape regarding emptiness in Nāgārjuna. Marcel Conche brings this out very directly: 'The nothing to which Pyrrho leads is an entirely different kind of nothing than the void that would simply be the opposite of being . . . It is not a matter of substituting nothingness for being as its opposite. Nor is it a matter of trying to preserve both, despite their opposition, by means of the notion of "becoming". In truth, for Pyrrho, what is at stake is a radical transformation of the philosopher's gaze – a completely different way of looking upon the totality of things. The Pyrrhonian nothing is neither pure nothingness nor non-being. One may call it . . . *τὸ φαινόμενον* (*phainómenon*).'[58]

What are things for Pyrrho, then? They are 'indifferent, unstable, and indeterminate'. Things are not fixed, they are not one, they are deprived of *ipseity*, they are not individuated – in fact, in his own gesture to co-becoming, Pyrrho holds that 'everything "is" only in relation'.[59] And yet things appear. And 'that which appears' or 'that which shows itself' is a *φαινόμενον*: a *phenomenon*. This is not a mere appearance juxtaposed to Being – a phenomenon *as opposed to a noumenon* – but rather a way of being characterized by the monotopic absence of any distinction between the two worlds.

Had Pyrrho been taken both literally and seriously, the entire history of Greek and European thought would be significantly different – and significantly more attuned to Indian or Chinese intellectual inclinations, as well as to several African[60] and Indigenous[61] philosophies where 'nothing pre-exists the relations that constitute it'.[62] Instead, Europe had to wait until the twentieth century for Pyrrho's ideas to become the cornerstone of a scientific revolution.

Ψ

The difference between *ontological* and *epistemic* scepticism can be seen at play in two of the founding figures of quantum mechanics: Niels Bohr and Werner Heisenberg.

As is well known, quantum physics undermines a core assumption of Western metaphysics: the idea that the world consists of separate entities, each with its own inherent and independently defined set of properties. As Niels Bohr would summarize in 1949: 'We are just faced with the impossibility, in the analysis of quantum effects, of drawing any sharp separation between an independent behaviour of atomic objects and their interaction with the measuring instruments which serve to define the conditions under which the phenomena occur.'[63] Measurement interactions are foundational, meaning that the choice of a specific measurement apparatus makes certain properties definite, while inherently excluding others. In other words, it is the combination or the relation of subject and object that individuates the object, which, scandalously, appears not to pre-exist the encounter as a determinate entity.

Both Bohr and Heisenberg shared this key insight of quantum theory. But, at least if we follow some interpretations of their arguments,[64] Heisenberg can be understood to place the accent on a *disturbance* caused by the measuring instruments on the measured particles, producing a modification of the measured object and hence limiting our capacity of knowing its real state. This would be an inherently *epistemic* limitation to our capacity of knowing the world – our knowledge of it is always marked by a 'principle of uncertainty'.[65] Bohr, instead, can be seen to insist that what is at stake is not merely a limitation to knowledge but a limitation to the actual state of things. Things are not inherently *determinate* but *uncertain*; rather, they are *indeterminate* to begin with – which amounts to saying they 'are' not – and are only *determinated*, or formed, through the process of establishing a relation to them, such as effecting a measurement.

According to Italian physicist Carlo Rovelli, quantum theory 'is the discovery that the properties of any entity are nothing other than the way in which that entity influences others. It exists only through its interactions.'[66] Reality cannot be discovered by human interpretation, but is fundamentally co-created. Nothing is determinate a priori, but all is the temporary determination, or, better, a determining, a forming, resulting from specific interactions and valid only within those interactions. We are part of the world we observe in the ontological sense that the particular part of the world we are observing *is* thus through its entanglement with us and our observation. In this sense, things *both are and are not*. This is the state of quantum *superpositions* and represents an ontological reading of indeterminacy that points to quantum theory's own tetralemma.[67]

Such reading breaks down the dualism of subject and object and hence the core *mediation* problematic of representationalism – how language, or subjectivity, can latch on to an external reality existing in-itself, objectively. The measurer and the measured are not pre-existing, autonomous entities that are bridged or mediated but, rather, co-arise in their horizontal encounter and there is nothing standing beyond that encounter.

That co-arising is what Bohr calls, echoing Pyrrho, a *phenomenon*. And as was the case with Pyrrho, phenomena are neither the appearance of something standing behind them (an appearance-*of*) nor do they merely refer to perceptions of the human mind or of consciousness (an appearance-*for*). Phenomena are, rather, the deletion of any distinction between appearance and reality, the melting away of an unnecessary convolution of the mind. And in this sense, as Karen Barad argues, 'phenomena are ontologically primitive relations – relations without preexisting *relata*'.[68] *Relata – things* – emerge through the relation.

This is an idea that emerges most clearly in contemporary relational quantum mechanics, as developed by Carlo Rovelli[69] and others. Any property only exists relative to another physical system with which it has interacted. This relational framework is what marks the context: the interaction of two systems and their constitution as subject and object at once *of* and *because of* the interaction. Removing the context removes the property: there's no 'view from nowhere' where a particle's spin is simply 'up' or 'down'. This is what Rovelli means when he says quantum states are not absolute descriptions of reality, but 'bookkeeping devices' for the correlations between systems.[70] The same quantum system can have different, even incompatible, states in different contexts – *without contradiction*, because each is defined relative to a different system, or in a particular *context*.

The original formulation of the principle of non-contradiction included reference to context: something, Aristotle argued, cannot both be and not be *in the same respect*. A road, for instance, can be uphill from Thebes and downhill from Athens, and both contradictory properties are true of it. Where Nāgārjuna's or Pyrrho's tetralemma and the relationality of quantum mechanics converge is in the expansion of the meaning of context – everything is at all times within a context, and any property that may be ascribed to a thing may only be so ascribed within such a context. In other words, there is no outside of the context (and any outside would merely become a *new* context). This is quite directly what Rovelli is arguing when he points out that in classical mechanics properties such as velocity or colour only have meaning with respect to another object, whereas in quantum mechanics 'the actual value of *all* physical quantities of *any* system is only meaningful in relation to another system. Value actualization is a relational notion like velocity.'[71]

The prosthetic mediation, which connects a subject to pre-existing individual entities, is replaced with the idea of a subject and an object concurring in the emergence of a phenomenon that retrospectively defines them both. Such an approach, of course, undoes the very ontological presumption at the basis of what Zhao Tingyang called 'dictionary thinking'. Things are not hovering in space, with their clearly defined properties and boundaries, waiting to be picked, studied and named. They emerge, rather, grammatically. That is to say, they emerge through the act of speaking them, or measuring them or relating to them. They are the outcome of a creation, or a *poiesis*, that operates and acquires a sense within a particular context.

Well beyond any anthropocentric reduction characteristic of subjectivist thought, the observer that determines the properties of the thing it observes is not necessarily a human, let alone a scientist, but is literally any one thing. Where Hegel states that 'the negative is the self',[72] there is here no Subject grounding the negativity of relational co-becoming. Objects interact one with the other, all the time and without any preferential position for a human subject.

This is how Rovelli reinterprets Bohr's idea of an observer: 'By using the word "observer" I do not make any reference to conscious, animate, or computing, or in any other manner special, system. I use the word "observer" in the sense in which it is conventionally used in Galilean relativity when we say that an object has a velocity "with respect to a certain observer". The observer can be any physical object having a definite state of motion . . . the observer can be a table lamp.'[73] Where Bohr spoke of the inseparability of 'atomic objects' from 'measuring instruments', we could rather speak of the inseparability of all things from their interaction with all others.

Quantum mechanics, so understood, is ultimately the discovery that the properties of objects are nothing other than the way each thing influences the other. This is why different observers can give different but true accounts of the same event, without that contradiction requiring that one be true and the other an illusion – the very meaning of event, of thing, ultimately of thing-event, encapsulates the multiplicity of its potentials.[74] A familiarity with the idea of the *monotopia* is what allows us to consider the most counterintuitive conclusions of quantum mechanics less scandalous. Or, in other words, the philosophical radicality of quantum theory is in large part due to its clash with acquired European metaphysical presuppositions. Presuppositions, as we have tried to show, that are widely disregarded in other parts of the world and in other histories than our own and that we could very well do without.

Bartleby's Principle

The idea of a *quantum universe* then points to a context that only makes sense from its interaction with an external observer. Any attempt at studying the whole requires that something be removed or separated from it, and hence the wholeness of the whole dissipates, transforming into a new context.[75] As Rovelli flatly tells us, 'to assume that it is in principle possible to list all the features of the world, all the values of all variables describing it at some fundamental level, at each moment of continuous time . . . is not possible'.[76] And where a 'uni-verse' quite literally refers to something that 'turns into one', the extension of the relational principle of velocity or colour to all things means that there can be no *one*, in fact no *everything* understood as a totality, for anything that turns (into a one) can only do so with respect to another, a *two*, standing outside of and not subsumed by it. This implies the impossibility of grasping any singular law or way, *logos* or *dao*,[77] that would mark the becoming of all.

In a beautiful fragment (B52), Heraclitus compares Time to a child playing and moving pieces on a board. But does it play according to certain rules that govern and thus are the totality? In answering negatively to the question, and hence radicalizing

Heidegger's reading of the fragment,[78] we echo first-century BCE Pyrrhonian philosopher Aenesidemus, who reinterpreted Heraclitean flux not as the manifestation of a rational cosmic order but as a contingent and unstable *fact*. Where Heraclitus saw contradiction and change as expressions of a deeper unity governed by reason, or the rules of the game played by Time, Aenesidemus strips this flux of metaphysical necessity, severing change from essence. Change is not a *logos* but merely a fact, not an essence of things but just what happens, or how things happen to stay – they stay in flux.[79]

Slavoj Žižek raises a familiar Aristotelian question in his engagement with Carlo Rovelli: 'When relational quantum mechanics posits that quantum events exist only in interactions and that the character of each quantum event is only relative to the system involved in the interaction . . . are these and similar claims universally true (true independently of any observer) or are they also valid only in relation to a specific (human) observer?'[80]

The only possible answer to this question is the famous rejoinder of Bartleby the scrivener when assigned work: *I would prefer not to.* Bartleby doesn't merely refuse – even a negative answer would still confirm the system and represent another instance of knowing what the world really is and is not like – but rather *withdraws* from meaning altogether. The only possible answer is an *abstention* from any claim to capture the whole. This awareness is a *predisposition* and not an object of knowledge. It is a *refraining-from*, an inclination to refuse to eternalize any one thing, truth or note, thereby closing all other options and having 'no eyes but for it'. Just like allusion is not approximation but restraining, this awareness is not positive knowledge – knowledge of the world, of how things truly are – but a negative realization that keeps alive a constant attitude of refusal. It is an embodied gesture. An *ethos*.

Where European philosophy begins its stupendous career as the 'first' science, the science that is above and prior to physics and to mathematics because it unearths 'that which always is',[81] and where that aspiration, following Kant's limitation of human access to reality, plunges into crisis, we can glimpse here a return of the primacy of thought *as an instrument of freedom*.

Bartleby's Principle functions as a limit, restraining the totalitarian temptations of the sciences, of technology and of course of philosophy itself. No singular *one* can rule – be it the descendant of a god, of a logical deduction, of a physical experiment or of a mathematical proof. Philosophy, which in Europe began its life as a delirious mania of primacy and exceptionality, returns today as the guardian against any primacy and any exceptionality. In that form, it returns as a guarantor of liberty. As a Republican philosophy censoring all imperial temptations and celebrating the freedom to create.

What is a thing?

Where Plato establishes the concept of Forms, the immutable Ideas that ground reality, we have tried to verbalize the concept, pointing to processes of formation. Things, ideas, perceptions or actions form in a *monotopia* or singular place without any original or truer ground beyond their temporary emergence. This approach is grammatical: it composes the world by rearranging things and producing additional meaning. It is creative. But what is the reality that emerges from indistinction and that assumes a form? What are the things that enter in relations? They aren't autonomous objects or atoms bestowed with an essential ipseity. And so, how are they cut out? Recalling Borges's poem, what is a tiger in the absence of anything that guarantees its unity and presence?

The answer is that an object is at the same time many objects. In a given context, the tiger may 'be' to me that sublime animal eliciting both fear and attraction, and quite specifically to *me*, with my metropolitan upbringing, that animal seen only ever in a zoo, inseparable in mind from the pungent smell of a captive beast in a cage. To someone else, call him Miguel, who has actually seen a tiger in the wild, whose great-grandparents worshipped a totemic tiger and not, like mine, a crucified immortal, the animal would be composed of a whole set of different associations – it is a beast that speaks of one's own identity and brings back the memory of stories heard in childhood. My tiger and Miguel's tiger overlap significantly but not wholly. We could certainly exchange views about the 'same' tiger, were we to spot an animal together, to the extent that 'same' identified a degree of relational similarity, a family resemblance that would appear as significant in the particular context of our exchange: it is, for both of us, a beast of prey; it is, for both of us, a striped animal, an endangered species, it inhabits the jungle and eats meat, including, possibly, us both. However, for a flea living on the tiger's fur, what we call tiger would have an entirely different consistency. It would be, probably, not even a *whole*, an entity graspable as an individuated totality, but a surface, or an environment. Very little communication would be possible between us two and the flea – perhaps only the existence of a form of matter that cannot be passed through, as a blockage of motion, or a support, a type of physicality or solidity. But yet again, the tiger in relation to a dog is once more a tangible whole, it elicits feelings of fear, and even if the dog shares none of my cultural references and has a very different sense from mine of the tiger's smell, we are nevertheless sufficiently aligned that, were we to meet a tiger, we would both run away from the same animal.

But then, is the tiger an object delimited in space, as it is for me, Miguel and the dog, or an unlimited environment, as it is for a flea that has never left its fur? Is it an object of abstraction, as it is for me and Miguel, or one of physical action-reaction, as it is for the two of us plus the dog? It is *all*, equally, and *neither*, essentially. Nāgārjuna's or Pyrrho's tetralemma, and quantum theory's own version of it in superposition, allows us to say that properties that are *real* need not be *absolute*, so that tiger-me is spatially distinct and tiger-flea is spatially indistinct and both properties are true even if they are contradictory. This is, equally, the deeper meaning of being-in-relation, or of the logic of co-becoming. Relationality is not a positive characteristic of things or of the world, but once more a principle of restraint or of abstention: I halt one step before assuming the ultimate closure of a thing that would make it uniquely *one*.

We discussed how traditional concepts of mediation lead to objects existing twice: once as our perception of it, the other as 'in itself' – *my* tiger, or 'the arrangement of human language', and the 'out of reach, flesh-and-bone tiger' out there. The type of self-constitutive relationality we are discussing here brings us instead to a world where there is neither *one* tiger nor *two*, but *infinite tigers*. With the caveat, however, that we are able to do to the dichotomy between *one* and *many* what we have done to that between *is* and *is-not*: an infinite set of tigers is the same as one tiger, the meaning of one is many, and the many constitute the one. This is what twentieth-century neo-Confucian philosopher Tang Junyi called the principle of *yiduobufenguan* (多不分觀), or 'one is many, many one',[82] whereby reality is neither reducible to a unity nor merely pluralistic, but rather consists of the inseparable interplay of unity and multiplicity. The tiger is a breathing, musical work of cadence.

The bottom line: we are not committed to defining and deciding, like a sovereign of the myriad things, like the author of a universal dictionary of all, how things are cut out. We are not land purveyors chartered to divide up Being and lay a thousand flags that say 'this is' on the thousand things, the way Adam did with the animals after creation. We are not the masters of relations, the creatures tasked with cutting them to shape. Rather, things emerge as one part of the world impacts another – and each part is therefore formed as it forms the effect of their interaction or co-becoming. So that, as Don

Quixote teaches Sancho Panza: 'What seems to you a barber's basin seems to me the helmet of Mambrino.'

Things are things *grosso modo*, literally *roughly cut*, they are just 'enough of *a* thing' (as opposed to many or infinite things) for a purpose. Flickering and unstable, things are things for the *productive* purposes at hand. They are sketched *while at work*, taking shape through what Chinese thought would call their *efficacy*, or their effect causing an action on and a reaction from the other particulars. The particular *organization*, the specific *context* of relations defines or individuates one thing as opposed to many. This context is nothing but the principle of *horizontal mediation* sharing the same ontological plane as that which it mediates, or the insubstantial organizing principle of the *monotopia*.

One may be reminded of Latour's actor network theory – whereby objects are actors, to the extent that they have an effect on other actor-objects. Not dissimilarly, Zhao Tingyang contrasts the Western *cogito*, centred on the 'I think' of a subjectivity faced with the possible existence of an external world, with what, drawing on eighteenth-century Italian philosopher Giambattista Vico, he terms the '*facio*' (I do) or '*creo*' (I make), where an object acquires an identity only by being locked in an interdependent relation with a subject. 'I create' reduces the space of the possible – it is a principle of individuation that, as we put it, proceeds *ex omnibus*. As Zhao phrases it: 'Infinity converges into limited possibilities within the constraints of positivity, and the infinitely dispersed possibilities must constantly converge into specific paths.' It is precisely this relational reduction or individuation of infinity into uniqueness or particularity that characterizes reality. And so, as Zhao concludes, 'to create is to create reality'.[83]

It is so that ontology, and ultimately philosophy itself, should not be understood as the *logos* of the *ontos*, or the science of Being, but rather as a way of creating and concentrating elements of reality so that they come into focus as a singular thing to one or more subjects. Verbalizing ontology, we obtain *ontopoiesis*.

Natural and artificial intelligence

Once we learn to look for it, creativity, production and recursive transformation are all around us. In biology, symbiogenesis designates a fundamental reorientation of evolutionary thought. In contrast to classical Darwinian frameworks that often conceive organisms as discrete units adapting to a pre-given environment, it understands living beings as the historically stabilized outcome of relations that were once external and contingent. As Lynn Margulis famously argued, the emergence of complex life cannot be explained solely through gradual variation and selection acting on isolated lineages, but involves enduring symbiotic incorporations that redefine what counts as an organism at all.[84]

Symbiogenetic perspectives undermine the ontological singularity of both 'individual' and 'environment'. Each emerges through processes that recursively transform the conditions of their own persistence. Recursivity stands for a structural feedback in which the effects of a process re-enter as conditions for its continuation – as when oxygenic photosynthesis creates an oxygen-rich atmosphere, which in turn enables new forms of life. Evolution thereby becomes less a matter of adaptation to fixed parameters than a continuous metamorphosis.[85] This insight animates James Lovelock's well-known Gaia hypothesis, which, stripped of its more organicist metaphors, articulates a tightly coupled system in which biological and geophysical processes co-constitute one another in a recursive entanglement between life and its conditions.[86]

Natural selection then operates on relational configurations rather than isolated entities. What persists are not organisms alone, but assemblages of organisms, environments and material processes that recursively stabilize one another. Bruno Latour has emphasized that such assemblages dissolve the classical distinction between organism and milieu, replacing linear causality with chains of mutual conditioning.[87] Evolution can then be seen as a process of collective transformation rather than unilateral adaptation.

Recursivity thus becomes not only a biological principle but an ontological one: it describes how forms of life generate, stabilize and govern the conditions of their own existence. Quite literally, permanence, or staying, only emerges through and in transformation. A thing is a thing in a context not merely in the perspectival sense of its being accessed and hence defined in a particular relational entanglement, but quite directly because the coming into being *of both thing and context* is only possible through their encounter (again – relation prior to *relata*).

Similarly, in brain development and function the concept of *epigenesis* refers to the idea that the brain's structure and capacities are not fully pre-specified by genes but *come into being* over time through dynamic interactions between genetic potentials, neural activity, bodily processes and environmental experience. Neural circuits are progressively constructed, modified and stabilized through development, learning and plasticity, rather than simply unfolded from a fixed genetic blueprint. Catherine Malabou calls this *ontogenesis*, or the *generation of being* through a recursive exchange between genes and environment, in a biological condition in which social or cultural environment can *mark the brain*, what it *is*, even more profoundly than a genetic alteration.[88]

This is, equally, how contemporary artificial intelligence operates, at least since it gained the ability to change its *being* by adapting to environmental changes in real time through processes of recursive co-production. A large language model, for instance, is first subjected to the foundational operation known as tokenization, or the segmentation of text into the 'tokens' the model can manipulate. Then the model enters training. Through prolonged exposure to large-scale datasets, it gradually constructs a geometry in which each token acquires meaning through its relations to others. For readers unfamiliar with machine learning, one might imagine this as a multidimensional conceptual map in which proximity corresponds to similarity and distance corresponds to divergence. Tokens that frequently appear in similar contexts cluster together; tokens that appear in contrasting situations drift apart. The model receives no instruction concerning what entities *are,* but rather discovers patterns in how they are used. Over time, this process yields an emergent structure. Concepts acquire a kind of internal existence defined as positions within a relational field that can influence the model's behaviour.

This provides what we might call a minimal technical sense of ontology: within the model, a distinction 'exists' to the extent that it is encoded in parameters and capable of shaping the model's outputs. But this existence remains purely potential. It becomes effective only when activated through the procedural and institutional layers that govern interaction. Through that interaction, words and concepts emerge or appear.

That coming-forth, that emergence from potentiality into actuality, can then reach back inward to reshape the model's internal individuation. Reinforcement Learning from Human Feedback (RLHF), for example, translates human value judgements – themselves shaped by annotation guidelines, cultural norms, market incentives and regulatory pressures – into weight updates that permanently alter the model's internal geometry. Instruction tuning performs a similar function; it exposes the model to curated examples of 'good behaviour', thereby reshaping the latent structure. These constitute a new round of heteronomous individuation, in which the model's internal structure is recursively reshaped by external normative regimes.

The model is then not a static object but a site of symbiotic individuation, in which distinctions are constantly produced, expressed, interpreted and reincorporated into the conditions of their own production. Through the generation of synthetic data and the recursive feedback of reinforcement learning, the model contributes to a shifting 'atmosphere' of information that subsequently feeds back into its own weight updates, refining its internal geometry in response to a field partly of its own making. This process dissolves the classical distinction between the internal 'being' of the model and the external 'environment' of its training data, revealing instead a site of symbiotic individuation where the model's latent ontology and the curated interactions of its users co-evolve. The ontopoietic hypothesis, with its emphasis on the creation of being, its *genesis* or *poiesis,* allows us to better understand what is happening all around us.

But unlike biological symbiogenesis, the recursive loops governing large language models are externally and *explicitly* designed. The feedback is mediated by data-curation protocols that are institutionally and normatively constrained. These determine what interactions are logged, which are discarded, how they are filtered for safety or quality, how annotators label them and which are selected for future finetuning. These curatorial practices determine which appearances become part of the model's future ontology, thereby shaping the next cycle of individuation. In this sense, the recursivity of large language models makes explicit something that remains merely implicit in the more complex biological symbiogenesis: there are *organizing principles* that guide the individuation of things and their creative transformation.

Ontopoiesis is guided by principles of organization, or what we termed horizontal mediation. We will now call these *protocols,* as our attention turns to the 'how' that governs what always flickers between one and many, between a barber's basin and the helmet of Mambrino.

Politics as First Philosophy

Protocols

In the dialogue *La Moda e la Morte*, early nineteenth-century Italian poet and philosopher Giacomo Leopardi stages a dialogue in which Fashion reveals itself as an ontological architect and Death's closest ally.

Fashion is shown to construct the very terms of existence. Like Death, it governs bodies, dictates suffering and lengthens or shortens lives by shaping trends such as hygienic standards, discomfort, self-harm or suicide. Unlike Death, however, Fashion does not kill directly; it seduces the living into collaborating in their own degradation, making them desire what weakens or destroys them. Where Death rules by necessity, Fashion rules by persuasion.

Control over forms of existence – how bodies move, dress, endure pain and value themselves – means power over life and death. The world we experience is filtered through the mandates of Fashion; our sense of time, value and even our own finitude is shaped by its cyclical decrees. In this sense, Fashion can be said to be an ontopoietic machinery; it literally creates the conditions of possibility for the conduct of a particular form of life.

A concept to refer to a fashion that becomes an ontopoietic device can be *protocol* – a word that has made a recent comeback in the age of digital decentralized governance, blockchain and artificial intelligence. According to one of many and overlapping definitions, a protocol is a set of explicit or implicit rules or procedures intended to govern, guide or influence conduct in a way that allows the emergence or construction of coordinated behaviour.[1] Protocols go by plenty of other names: norms, laws, standards, customs, traditions, contracts, commands, regulations, manners, morals, values, expectations, and so on.

The classical example of protocol as codified behaviour that retreats into invisible habit is hand-washing. As Leopardi's Fashion would quickly point out, the existence of a widespread hygienic habit enables the survival of millions of lives that would be lost to easily controllable pathogens if the correct washing protocol were to go out of fashion.

The bottom line is that a protocol is not merely a guide to action but is itself constitutive of a certain productivity. This comes out clearly in contemporary art. *Protocolism*[2] names an orientation in artistic practice that uses protocols to guide human and nonhuman practitioners in the production of unique artworks, so that rules, procedures and relational systems become the primary site of production. The artist functions as a system architect who designs an autonomous field of operations to dictate how artworks reproduce over time. It is the decentralized code defining the protocol, rather than any single output, that becomes the locus of creativity, marking a shift in the ontology of the artwork from the finished object to the underlying logic of its generation. The tradition of participatory or relational aesthetics, in which the public engages with and hence gives life to the artwork through prescribed actions, is here given an ontopoietic shift: participation does not engage *with* or *in* a singular artwork, but it is rather *productive* of multiple works through a protocol that becomes at once an artwork and an explicit condition of possibility for other artworks.

Artists Holly Herndon and Mat Dryhurst, for example, have developed a practice that challenges classical categories of authorship and artistic production by foregrounding the rules, infrastructures and collective systems through which works come into being. In the installation *The Call* at London's Serpentine Gallery, rather than presenting a finished artwork, they composed a sequence of protocols. Fifteen choirs from across the United Kingdom performed a bespoke songbook created for the project and these performances became a dataset that would feed into generative choral models whose voices filled the gallery constantly, producing new derivative artworks. The work also experimented with a 'data trust', a mechanism designed to redistribute ownership and agency over the training data back to the singers who produced it. The artwork was the system or *dispositif* through which voices were collectively transformed, rather than the sonic outputs alone.

Herndon and Dryhurst carried these ideas further in *Starmirror* at Berlin's KW Institute for Contemporary Art (2025). Here the exhibition space became an open protocol experiment, inviting visitors and choirs into live call-and-response interactions with AI models trained on human voices. The installation emphasized iteration over closure: systems were not displayed as completed objects but as ongoing procedures subject to participation. That shift from object to process, from artefact to world, captures a central intuition of protocolism: artworks can be generative environments or poietic devices.

Protocol art can be most clearly understood when read in its relation with conceptual art. In his famous *One and Three Chairs* (1965), Joseph Kosuth demonstrated that an artwork need not reside in a material object, but could consist in a conceptual proposition, articulated through the relation between an object, its image and its linguistic definition. Meaning is produced discursively and stabilized through institutional and interpretive contexts such as the museum, the catalogue or the art world.

Take, in contrast, the work of one of the pioneering figures of protocol art, Pak. Pak inherits Kosuth's primacy of the idea, but displaces it into a computational and protocol-based register. In *The Title* (2021), Pak presents a series of NFTs (non-fungible tokens) that all point to the same visual file – a rotating digital cube – while differing only in their on-chain titles, prices and modes of distribution. Here, as with Kosuth, the image is deliberately stripped of aesthetic privilege, and what matters is the conceptual distinction introduced by language. Yet, unlike Kosuth's work, these distinctions are not merely stated but acquire an ongoing generativity. When a protocol is executed, it doesn't replicate or enact an existing work, but generates an entirely new creation, blurring and diffusing concepts of authorship and even copyright.[3] The difference between 'The Cheap', 'The Expensive', or 'The Unsold' is not an interpretive gesture, but an executable condition that governs ownership, circulation and value in real time. The concept becomes inseparable from its technical instantiation or immanent realization. The 'statement' of the artwork is no longer a proposition to be contemplated but a logic to be entered, one that produces consequences through participation.

The individual artwork as outcome of a given protocol is not a finished entity but an event – a momentary resolution of a procedural field, or, as we argued earlier, a stop, a malfunction even, upon which a temporary closure is grounded, letting a thing appear. What exists is what emerges from the execution of a particular protocol under specific conditions. The artwork becomes a site where composable rule-sets produce emergent realities that show as artistic phenomena in Niels Bohr's sense: a product of a distributed apparatus rather than the expression of an underlying substance.

In his celebrated study of decentralized digital systems, Alexander Galloway claims that protocol is how *control* exists after decentralization.[4] Control here is nothing but an organizing principle, or a horizontal mediation that is made explicit and denuded in its created and creative contingency (*this* protocol, *that* organization). Protocols offer a conceptual lens through which the procedural organization of life becomes intelligible. They make visible a field of potentials, or a structured set of constraints that define the possible trajectories of individuation. Truth does not pre-exist the identification of the criteria for its own definition. The site of contestation, and of ontopoietic creation, transitions from the level of defining what is true and what is false to defining the rule, what counts as true and what counts as false, or the protocol. Protocols, in short, are what transform *yiduobufenguan* (多不分觀), the one-and-many, into one or multiples ones, or what reduces infinity to concretized existence. They are the created and creative principles of *creatio ex omnibus*.

Truth under protocol

In a short book on the concept of universality, contemporary philosopher Sun Ge recounts her experience as a Chinese citizen in a German city. Returning home in the evening along an empty street, she inadvertently started walking on the bike lane that ran parallel to the pavement. No bicycles were in sight. And yet, another lonely passer-by reproached her for walking on a path reserved for bicycles. This, Sun Ge was curtly informed, is against the rules. From this common German experience – one that appears as unreadable to Mediterranean as it does to Chinese eyes – Sun Ge is led to reflect on the different predispositions of common sense. In China, she says, everyone would have understood that no harm was done in walking on an empty bike lane. In Germany, on the other hand, what mattered was not the contingent, empirical reality of the act, but the fact that it represented a breach of the law. This anecdote frames her distinction between categorial imperatives and dynamic contextual analysis, or universality and particularity.

In the continuation of her text, Sun Ge calls for the employment of 'empirical reason' to guide the emergence of a singular action or belief through an analysis of what the situation at hand requires. To clarify her point, she narrates a story from sixteenth-century Ming philosopher and *enfant terrible* Li Zhi, who wrote two essays dealing with similar cases from which however he drew opposite conclusions. The first essay involves a monk named Ruowu who has an old, widowed mother with two kids. Ruowu, in furtherance of his meditation, plans to travel to Vajra Mountain to practise religion as a hermit. His mother writes him a letter opposing his plan, saying that if he was truly devoted to religion, he could practise it anywhere, be it Vajra Mountain or at home. Li Zhi speaks highly of this mother commenting that 'great mother at home, the Buddha under your knees'. The second case is about Huan An, who decides to resign from his political career and withdraw from secular life to practise Buddhist ideals while also leaving his widowed mother at home. But this time, as the purpose of his decision is to repay his mother's love and care, Li praises him for being exemplary in filial piety.

In both cases, the son is a monk who leaves his widowed mother to practise religion. Both are unable to meet the direct responsibility of filial piety to take care of their old mothers. Li Zhi, however, has very contrasting remarks on the two. And here is the moral that Sun Ge draws from the story: 'Removed from concrete circumstances and experiences, "becoming Buddha" could not gain its independent significance.'[5]

For Sun Ge knowledge is entangled within a particular organization of meaning and only acquires a sense within a delimited context.[6] If, in quantum mechanics, the context refers to the encounter between observer and observed, and in the very particular instance of a subatomic experience to the encounter of the scientist and a particle through the instruments of observation, in situations where larger and combined phenomena are under discussion the context broadens to include multiple disturbances and relations.[7]

A context is always defined or cut out from the point of view of another context for which it becomes the object of observation. What we have termed Bartleby's Principle relinquishes the possibility of a singular totality, or of a one without a two – any object as much as any context emerges as such only with respect to an outside, to another one. In this sense, a context, to the extent that it is individuated as a context and hence that it is, is always a context for a purpose, one defined by its efficacy, anchoring the reason for which the context has been individuated in the first instance. It follows, then, that a context is both creative and created. It is to underline this dual nature, this purposiveness and agential promise, that we choose to employ the word *protocol* to define such a sense-making context that is itself made. Recalling Zhao Tingyang, a protocol transforms our understanding of reality from one based on *ego cogito* to one based on *ego facio*.

Take, for instance, Guy Debord's concept of the *dérive*. Advanced within Situationist theory, the *dérive* calls for a drifting guided by the compelling allure of ambiance. Freed from predetermined destinations, participants immerse themselves in the psycho-geographical currents shaping city life. This entails an exploration of urban spaces that bypasses conventional modes of orientation in favour of unexpected encounters and heightened awareness.

The process of *flânerie*, similarly, calls us to observe the city's ebb and flow with detached curiosity, seeking pleasure in unexpected details and fleeting encounters. Strolling becomes a form of aesthetic exploration, revealing hidden social patterns and the poetic dimensions of mundane life. Paris literally *speaks* to Baudelaire's *flâneur.* Walter Benjamin *listens* to the streets of Naples.

In both of these practices, the truth procedure generating the outcome is presupposed in the type of protocol defining the meaning and consequence of orientation; it is right and propitious to get lost and to discover something unusual, and it is *not* right and propitious to chart the path of least opposition and easiest arrival. Both *dérive* and *flânerie* operate according to a principle of orientation, but of a quite different kind from the one that would help a trekker find their way out of the forest.

In protocol-based art, each instantiation of a generative artwork is equally legitimate because legitimacy follows from correct execution of the rule-set rather than from proximity to an original form. And yet, just as in the case of the *flâneur* or the situationist explorer, this does not imply mere randomness. Protocols are structured and often highly constrained. They provide a rationality that is non-universal yet non-arbitrary, sets of rules that generate worlds without claiming to be the whole world.[8] And so, just as a furry environment was the true answer to the question 'what is a tiger-flea', very different directions are equally true answers to the *different* questions concerning 'movement-*dérive*', 'movement-*flânerie*' and 'movement-instrumental'.

Without a protocol, 'becoming Buddha' could not gain its independent significance.

A protocol individuates meaning (体用)

We will now further stretch the concept of protocol and redefine it as an assemblage of particulars each temporarily stabilized as *one same thing for a subject.* To decide what befits a *flânerie,* for instance, I must individuate the meaning of movement, of city, of unexpected encounter, and myriad other particulars that together contribute to defining the protocol in which *flânerie* can take up meaning as a practice. Whether it is a man roaming Paris or running away from a tiger, a flea deciding where to jump, a fire burning a candle or a monk deciding a course of action, a set of actions/reactions, of things-in-relation, must be delimited to yield the action or let *one solution* come into focus. These things must be *given a name*, not merely in a linguistic sense, but in the sense of each being individuated as *one* as opposed to *many*; they must be *stabilized*. In this sense, we could consider a protocol as a situated, concrete and factually creative version of Foucault's broad concept of a *dispositif*, 'a thoroughly heterogeneous ensemble consisting of discourses, institutions, architectural forms, regulatory decisions, laws, administrative measures, scientific statements, philosophical, moral and philanthropic propositions – in short, the said as much as the unsaid'.[9]

Consider again Sun Ge's sentence: 'Removed from concrete circumstances and experiences, "becoming Buddha" could not gain its independent significance.' We should take this both seriously and literally. Without a protocol, 'becoming Buddha' is *insignificant* in the sense that it does not exist as *a* thing but is left oscillating between everything and nothing. The protocol creates the conditions of possibility for both being and signification. In this sense, the protocol individuates and concretizes a signified that does not exist and did not pre-exist outside of itself.

Alexander Galloway defines protocols as 'a universal description language for objects', but he then goes on to add that 'a protocol does not produce or causally effect objects, but rather is a structuring agent that appears as the result of a set of object dispositions'.[10] And here we would rather say the opposite: *the disposition of things is synonymous with their production or with their being* to the extent that things do not pre-exist their placement and organization but *are* their placement and organization. Relations nurturing *relata*, with things assuming a specific form through their usage.

Classical European philosophy often treats form as the essence of a thing-in-itself, with function relegated to a secondary, derivative role – what the thing does after it has been constituted. Chinese thought provides a striking alternative. Within much of its tradition,[11] form and function (*ti-yong* 體用) are not sequential but simultaneous – mutually implicating moments of a single, dynamic process. The question is not merely what hidden structure underlies appearance, but how an underlying pattern is made manifest through its efficacy. Static identity gives way to operative realization. In this view, 'what something is' cannot be severed from 'how it works'. Form is discerned through action, and action is intelligible only as the realization of a pattern. This intimacy between structure and operation helps account for the characteristic continuity in Chinese philosophy between moral cultivation, political order and metaphysics. We here employ the term 'protocol' to signify a similar ontological unity of form and function.

This amounts, ultimately, to reiterating something we have seen earlier at play in the constitution of things: everything acquires meaning and truth value within a context. Their being-situated, their being-in-relation, ultimately their acquiring a particular type of orientation within a cartography: this is not a subjectivist diminution of a higher form of being, but the very being of being-there as being-in-position. Removing protocol or context from a particular does not result in a liberated and autonomous object but in a dead thing that is no longer there. Without protocol there is, simply, nothing, or, what amounts to the same thing, everything. The protocol is not a-ontological, an epistemic human addendum that cages us in a language game distinct from reality, but rather *ontopoietic*, or *creative of being* in the one and only sense and place.

This is one of the characteristics distinguishing *ontopoiesis* from pragmatism. It is not merely that we all happen to have a similar relation to a certain thing, but rather the opposite: the thing exists as one thing and not many because we have a similar relation to it. A protocol summons into being a specific thing that manifests itself as *the same thing* for the involved subjects. Protocols enable *communication* in its etymological sense of 'making common', allowing the infinite variability of things to recede and to become stabilized.

Communication does not only mean language: think of ants that rush to carry the *same fly* to the *same hive*. Or a forest where trees interact with fungal networks that braid roots together, transferring nutrients from one to another and warning of predators, so that each organism is a node in a web that allows the community to persist, displaying, on some accounts, behaviours that question any strict mind–body dichotomy.[12] The same applies to artificial systems: think of distributed networks, where nodes can directly communicate one with the other without mediation by a centre because they share the same protocol. And we can extend this to the most infinitesimal matter, in the sense given by relational quantum mechanics to the idea of an exchange of information within a quantum system, where the fact that two observers can appear to see 'the same object' is explained by chains of correlations and communication events between them. For Observer A, the object is defined by the outcomes of A's interactions with it; for Observer B, by B's outcomes. When A and B interact, they form new relations between themselves. If quantum theory predicts that the results in these new relations are highly correlated, then A and B will agree they have seen the 'same' outcome. The appearance of a unified, shared object is therefore the persistence of consistent correlations across multiple relational networks; form is stabilized function.[13]

The subjects of a *dérive* or of a *flânerie* all participate in the same protocol to the extent that they all see *sufficient same things* to organize it as a meaningful space of interaction and not a space of incommunicability – such as agreeing on what non-instrumental movement and urban exploration *are*. The constellation of particulars inhabited by the two monks mentioned by Li Zhi includes philosophical attitudes and moral predispositions, such as the meaning and importance of filial piety, that are understood because they are individuated as the same thing for all. It defines a type of discourse that is meaningful to all as *the same type* of discourse: deciding what a monk should do means deciding a course of action and not, say, drawing a painting of the act of decision-making. These particulars, together with many others such as the monks having a mother and a sufficiently shared perception of the meaning of being-mother, their position as monks, and literally a multitude of other individuations or distinctions that contribute to the protocol acquiring sense and hence ontological creativity: all these particulars provide the ground for a judgement to emerge. *It really could not be in a better way*, argues the judge who resolves the protocol of which they are a part.

In a sense, a protocol is an infinite cartography. Quite literally everything, ultimately and in some form, contributes to everything else if we zoom in deep enough. The very creative actions *on* a protocol are only conceivable *within* another protocol, making those actions intelligible in the first place. The content of any protocol is always another protocol; its extension is marked by fractal boundary. As mathematician Benoît Mandelbrot demonstrated,[14] the answer to the question 'How long is Britain's coastline?' depends on the measuring stick. A large unit skips tiny curves, giving a shorter length, while zooming in closer reveals countless new details, lengthening the measurement. Mandelbrot showed that natural boundaries are fractal: their complexity is endless, making their length indeterminate. But just as measuring a boundary implies choosing a stick and a level of granularity, thereby *individuating* a length and *foreclosing* other possibilities, so a protocol must be defined by delimiting the extension of what counts as relevant information to stay within the protocol and to let it emerge as *a* or *one* protocol in the first instance.

A protocol is always a cartography for a purpose, or a partial but creative whole that emerges by bracketing out or ignoring other relations. Defining and hence delimiting a protocol is then both an act of *optical* focus in the sense Ames gives to the expression 'Zhongyong' (中庸 the *mean*) and of *political* focus in the sense that it identifies those things that count or have value for yielding a result.

Without a measuring stick, or graduated lenses, or a protocol, there is no 'length in itself': there is, simply, nothing, or, what amounts to the same thing, everything. Delimiting a protocol is the optical limitation that enables the possibility of vision. It is not only philosophers who begin by 'plucking out their eyes'; this is how reality constitutes itself.

A protocol creates a subjectivity

Just as a protocol stands for the individuation and stabilization of a thing that appears as the same thing to a multiplicity, so, conversely, a protocol individuates that multiplicity as a *subjectivity* and not a mere collection of individualities.

The bee appears (is created) as the same bee to many ants, *and hence* the ants appear (are created) as a group knit together by having a relation to that same thing understood as something to be hunted, carried and eaten. Just as a thing becomes the same thing to many, so the many, through their recognition of others' perception of the same thing, emerge not as merely juxtaposed singularities but as a common subject to the extent they are all *subjected* to the same thing.

This is a process we have seen at play with the Chinese expression *you* (有), which means 'to have' but refers to something that 'there is', hence grammatically installing the fact that anything that is summons a subject that has or contains it. Of course, subject individuations that have a chance of lasting and acquiring a meaning in both the linguistic and evolutionary sense require an entire cartography of overlapping contexts. If a 'group' communicating the same 'thing' was identified merely by the fact of hunting, carrying and eating that same fly, then ants would appear indistinguishable from beetles; they would form a single subject (which, at a broader level of granularity, they do – the biological class of insects).

Hartmut Rosa's sociology of human relationships posits that both subject and world are constituted in and through their mutual relatedness, which, with an unacknowledged turn to Chinese grammar, he terms resonance: 'As Maurice Merleau-Ponty in particular never tires of noting, it is through the effect of gravity on our body, the working of our senses, and the tactility of our skin that a palpable world first emerges, and with it every form of consciousness as consciousness and perception of the presence of something not only to which the experiencing subject finds itself related, but which is constitutive of experience and thus of the subject itself. If we accept this notion of a fundamental relatedness that precedes the division of subject and object and serves as the very basis both of the presence of world and of subjective experience, then resonance appears not as something that first develops between a self-conscious subject and a 'premade' world, but as the event through which both commence.'[15]

There is no reality *for* a subject that is not at once ontopoietically created *by* and *in* the interpretation, and there is no subject without a reality to which it is both subjected and creatively engaged. Reality is 'interpretation' in the sense given to the term in theatre, where a stage character exists only to the extent that it is interpreted: Hamlet appears only through the actor who plays him. Actor and part co-arise in the act of interpretation, and, more fundamentally still, it is the act itself that gives them meaning. Without interpretation, there is no actor and no role, only a human and words on a page.

The word interpretation originates in a practice of mediation. Its Latin root, *interpres*, designates an intermediary: a translator, a broker or an arbiter who stands in-between and makes exchange possible. To interpret is to bring something into circulation, to render signs or actions intelligible and authoritative for others. Interpretation is an act that operates in public space: it stabilizes meaning by situating it within a shared framework where it can have effects.

This mediating role carries a creative and evaluative dimension. The *interpres* does not merely transmit a pre-existing meaning, but actively confers form and value – much as a broker assigns a price that allows an object to enter an economy. In this abstract sense, interpretation 'prices' meaning: it gives a sign a determinate standing as something rather than nothing. What is uninterpreted is nonexistent; what is interpreted becomes operative, actionable and subject to protocols.

It is through a common interpretation that a community is formed. Gramsci repeatedly argues that collective subjects such as classes, peoples or nations do not exist as fully formed entities prior to their political mobilization. Workers did not exist as a class before the solidarities and conflicts of the labour movement constituted them as *interpres* of a reality. Anticolonial revolutions, as Fanon observed, forged the colonized into a people through practices of revolt that reframed the position of subalternity. And, as Cornelius Castoriadis reminds us, society constitutes itself through a power deeper than laws and constitutions – a creative and institutive imagination that invents the very terms of its order.[16] That power is ontopoietic interpretation. Subjects and objects arise together in a way that may remind us of the Baron of Munchausen, who famously and impossibly lifted himself up by pulling on his own hair.

Protocols are then continually transformed through new acts of interpretation, reconfiguring the conditions under which subject and object meet and reshaping both. All protocols are forged within a world already crowded with interpretations, with existing cartographies that structure perception and practice. To succeed, a new proposition must persuade against the inertia of established forms, ushering in new functions and hence new forms. In some epochs, shifting perception required extraordinary force: the decree of an absolute monarch to bend Egyptian art into Akhenaten's elongated forms, or the collective insistence of Renaissance composers to free polyphony from ecclesiastical restraint. Once a new way of focusing a part of reality gains ground and summons its subjectivity, it sediments into habit. What began as a daring interpretation becomes, once repeated and adopted, the new way of seeing, hearing or acting, ultimately the *habitus* that maintains a community.[17]

Conversely, when the tenability of communication breaks down within a protocol, a different disposition of particulars is called for – a recalibration of the subject–object context through a rectification of either or both. Take, for instance, extreme political polarization in the United States under President Donald Trump, whereby words such as 'free speech' or even 'democracy' come to mean very different things to different people, thereby splintering a national community into separate tribes standing guard one against the other. This is what anchors Confucius' call for the 'rectification of names', so that a ruler who does not rule justly *is not* a ruler, or a son who is not filial *is not* a son. Xunzi sharpened this into a political technology: names are conventions that must be codified if institutions are to endure.

That codification is the instrument of seeing with the same eyes and hence organizing a community. To see in the same way means precisely not to see that one sees in the same way, but inhabiting that condition as a sensitivity and sensibility, an inclination that becomes the tacit *ça va sans dire* of communal life. Zhuangzi puts it starkly: 'Life is in mutual forgetting.'[18] What has been internalized disappears into habit, and in so doing realizes the full capacity of encounter between subject and object, each forming the other through practice. Confucian thought describes this as ritual cultivation, 'a strategy for orchestrating the communicating community into its fullest consonance, with appropriately disposed members resonating productively in their social transactions'.[19] Rituals are protocols that individuate subjects as they bind communities into coherence. To act outside ritual is not simply to be immoral, but to be *incorrect* – to have fallen outside the shared focus that constitutes a specific instance of humanity and of that which is.[20]

And yet. Are we ever able to move beyond *a specific instance* of humanity? If a protocol creates its own community, do we then have to accept the tribe and the fragment as the only organizing principle of our world?

Hemispheres

Just like a body-politic encompasses the different parts of a polity but is pitted against other communities, so a protocol may be seen to create its own fiefdom, standing guard against all others. Where, for Carl Schmitt, every law is bound to a concrete order rotating around a sovereign,[21] we risk having to admit that every truth is bound to a protocol rotating around a community. This is the world of *Hémisphères*, Tristan Garcia's philosophical short story painting a future where humanity has fractured into secluded bubbles, hemispheric protocols, each inhabited by like-minded people.[22]

Does the lack of a ground mean that any emergence remains merely arbitrary, any choice the product of the vagaries of love, whimsical, ultimately equivalent to any other choice we may have made, and so all stays relative and equally absurd? Are we returned to a place of multiple civilizational and algorithmic bubbles, each with their own equivalent values and truth procedures?[23]

This is the question that will guide us from now on: is *ontopoiesis* capable of nurturing a general organizing principle functioning as a kernel for the articulation of principles, norms and truths guiding diverse peoples and perhaps even diverse species, or does it precipitate us in a walled world of philosophical multipolarity or multimodality, where each pole indifferently resonates as it pleases?

The ethos of universality

One of the last essays written by Michel Foucault examines Kant's response to the question 'What is Enlightenment?'. One would expect Foucault to be disdainful of Kant's approach. The Enlightenment juxtaposes the arbitrary imposition of the will of authority onto the immature with the autonomous quest for truth of the mature. Foucault should argue that no such distinction can be made: all claims to truth are ultimately claims of or to power and authority, made by and for the benefit of someone. The imposed discourse of the king and the rebellious discourse of the enlightened bourgeoisie are antithetical but comparable truth procedures. And yet, Foucault chooses to focus on another aspect of Kant's essay. 'The thread that may connect us with the Enlightenment', he writes, 'is not faithfulness to doctrinal elements, but rather the permanent reactivation of an attitude – that is, of a philosophical ethos that could be described as a permanent critique of our historical era.'[24] The Enlightenment for Foucault is first and foremost an attitude and an inclination; it is a process that exists only to the extent that humans engage in and practise it.

Immanuel Kant never claimed that his times were *enlightened*; rather, he claimed they were times *of enlightenment*, with the torch of reason carried by concrete individuals. The specification points to a continuous process of shedding light: a dynamic task as opposed to a fixed state.[25] With a grammatical turn applied to the noun, nothing is enlightened until it is lit. We might recall our earlier mention of Hamlet in Foucault's comment: 'Thus Enlightenment must be considered both as a process in which men participate collectively and as an act of courage to be accomplished personally. Men are at once elements and agents of a single process. They may be actors in the process to the extent that they participate in it; and the process occurs to the extent that men decide to be its voluntary actors.'[26]

The question then becomes: what sets the ethos of Enlightenment apart from other activities – for instance, prayer? It surely cannot be having truth in its immutable essence as the promise of correct philosophizing: no such thing exists for Foucault. Those engaged in the process of Enlightenment, he tells us, try to answer the following question: 'In what is given to us as universal, necessary, and obligatory what place is occupied by whatever is singular, contingent, and the product of arbitrary constraint?'[27] They attempt to denude the claims to universality, eternity and immobility of an enunciation to show its particular, contingent and relative nature.

Foucault's own critical project can be understood as the unearthing of dominant protocols, unveiling, for instance, the contingent and situated practices governing and hence defining sexuality (literally, giving it closure, hence making it into something as opposed to everything and nothing). And yet, one can step beyond mere critique, simple relativizing, the dissolution of proudly held beliefs in ironic laughter. Armed with the awareness of the particularity, contingency and relativity of the enunciation, concept or historical situation they critique, those interpreting the ethos of the Enlightenment then attempt a 'possible transgression' of their historical moment, signalling 'the possibility of no longer being, doing, or thinking what we are, do, or think' and, in so doing, giving 'new impetus, as far and wide as possible, to the undefined work of freedom'.[28]

Parrhesia – a type of speech that undermines the authority of its object of criticism – is accompanied by a reconstruction of sense and authority. Freedom is put to work for the re-creation of meaning, or the emergence of a new protocol that is seen to better resonate with the world in its particular time. We do not reach the immobility of an Aristotelian plant or Zhao Wen's aphonia, but we will be, do or think again and differently. In this sense, Foucault turns Kant's critical approach on its head: the question is no longer focusing on *that which we cannot know*, drawing a cartography of our limitations and raising *prohibition* to first philosophy, but rather uncovering *what else we may be*, opening the door not to restraint, but to the potential of creativity. Here lies the productive blindness: in being, when one should soon not be; in doing, when one's actions will soon be undone; in thinking, when one's thoughts will soon be transgressed anew.

Just as the ethos of Enlightenment rotates around its verbalization, we will now claim the same for universality. Transforming a hemispheric protocol into *a universal* interprets an ethos that aims to *universalize* and stretch it towards the impossible: a universal protocol guiding the individuation of given objects for *everyone everywhere* and hence concurrently summoning *a universal subject.*

This is, strictly speaking, meaningless well before impossible; as we have amply discussed, there is no such thing as an a-contextual totality or a context that sums up the entire universe. But what is really going on under the ethos of universality is the search for a protocol that would be adopted by everyone everywhere *for all practical and productive purposes invoked by the specific protocol one wishes to universalize.*

What lets a thing emerge as the same thing is a particular way of focusing a particular aspect of reality, of individuating it, enabling the communication of sufficiently similar results yielded by the relations of each of the interlocutors to the object and to each other. To aspire to universalize a thing means to aspire to create a common way of seeing for a given encounter or situation.[29]

As an example, we can here give a different spin to Gramsci's critique of Kant's golden rule. The categorical imperative is grounded, for Gramsci, in a complex web of institutional, material and social relations that individuate particular subjects sharing 'similar conditions'. Without these conditions of possibility, without this specific articulation of the cartography, Kant's universal law could not make sense to a communal, if delimited, subjectivity (to the European subjects of Enlightenment). And yet, the fact that an injunction such as Kant's categorical law only applies to individuals in similar conditions does not render the injunction a priori invalid. Rather, it *situates* it, unveiling the particular subjects that are individuated by that injunction (say, cosmopolitan European intellectuals). But subjects, and conditions, can and do change. And so we could really read Gramsci's critique not as a confutation of Kant's law, but as its transposition onto an immanent or monotopic plane, its transition from *logos* to *ethos*, and hence as an implicit injunction to *produce* those similar conditions for everyone everywhere *if* the universal is to apply.

We can see this logic at play in the famous injunction by Heidegger that 'the end of philosophy is the planetarization of European modernity', where *planetarization*, in its verbal modality, is akin to *universalization*. From its Greek inception, so goes the argument, philosophy sought to ground truth in what *is*. This trajectory culminates in the calculative rationality of modern technology. Philosophy's 'end' is thus its consummation: its reduction to techno-science. The global spread of this technical rationality is what Heidegger names 'planetarization'. A way of disclosing beings born in Europe – the will to order, calculate and dominate – now encompasses the whole globe. European modernity has succeeded, according to Heidegger's reading, in creating 'similar conditions' for everyone everywhere in their relation to technoscience: it has successfully universalized a fundamental existential protocol.

A universal is a thing that aims to appear as the same thing to a universal subject. The ethos of universality is the inclination to universalize, to try and create the conditions of possibility for a universal to emerge. Swapping *logos* for *ethos* means abandoning the quest for certainty and entering the domain of the normative, of the ethical, and of the political as a new form of transformative ontology; ultimately, the domain of *ontopoiesis*.

Persuasion

We can dig further into the ethos of universality by contrasting two apparently similar golden rules. The first is Kant's categorial imperative, which we have just discussed: 'Act only according to that maxim whereby you can at the same time will that it should become a universal law.' The second emerged in the period of the warring states in China, and it is Confucius' famous maxim on reciprocity: 'Do not impose on others what you yourself do not desire.'[30]

Kant critiqued the traditional principle of a golden rule of reciprocity for being too dependent on individual preferences. His own version focuses on whether the proposed action can be rationally willed as a principle for everyone to follow, making the rule a logical necessity whose truth is self-evident and unquestionable.

We could, however, read the Confucian maxim as an *invitation*. Grounded neither on individual preference nor on imperative reason, it extends an *offer* to follow a way considered resonant with the state of the world and to see things the same way.

The Chinese original – 己所不欲，勿施於人 – features the particle 所 (suǒ), which in classical Chinese precedes a verb to nominalize it, producing 'that which is [verb]-ed'. Here, 所不欲 does not mean 'do not desire (now)', but 'that which one does not desire (in general)'. The grammatical shift transforms a transient, situational aversion into a stabilized, generalized object. This nominalization universalizes the scope of the maxim: the standard is not a fleeting preference but a category of action or condition that one would reject if reversed. Linguistically, 所 embeds the movement from the particular to the universal within the sentence's very structure. It generalizes the object of 'not desiring', producing a stable-seeming category: 'that which one does not desire'. Accordingly, the subject of the sentence is neither 'me, Confucius' nor 'you, the reader', but a generic 己 (jǐ) – 'oneself'.

This may invite comparison with Western moral universalism, where universals presuppose fixed categories or essences. But, as we have seen, in classical Chinese thought there is no metaphysical *ousia* anchoring such stability. The paradox resolves when we see that Confucius' universalization is not ontological but ontopoietic. 所 does not freeze the undesired; it extracts from a concrete act *a repeatable relational pattern*. The universality advanced here is that of a *procedure*: whenever a comparable relation recurs, the maxim yields comparable results. The 'generalized object' is a linguistic–ethical tool, not a metaphysical constant; it is an instrument, a way of focusing, a protocol. As such, it achieves stability only at the level of practice or habit: ritualized social life gives continuity to the pattern, even as the content shifts with circumstances. That ritualized life is nothing but a principle of upkeep, or maintenance, or an ethos of universality allowing for the emerge of universals – such as the prohibition of murder.

Similar considerations can be seen at play in the concept of *Satyāgraha*, a neologism coined by Gandhi. Satyāgraha presupposes a world without epistemic sovereignty – a world in which no individual, creed or institution can legitimately claim privileged access to truth. Truth appears only in relation, as the provisional outcome of a shared inquiry conducted among agents who are mutually exposed and mutually fallible. This is why Gandhi situates the satyāgrahi not *opposite* an adversary, but *before* one, inviting the other into a dialogical process in which each party submits its convictions to the test of reciprocal recognition. Satyāgraha thus displaces the classical, monological idea of truth as an object to be possessed, and replaces it with truth as an event, a happening shaped by the ethical dispositions of those who seek it together.[31]

In more recent years, the work of biologist Michael Levin has introduced a framework that productively reorients fundamental philosophical questions about agency, influence and causation.[32] At its core, his work challenges a persistent conceptual binary: the division between mere mechanistic objects and autonomous, minded subjects. Levin posits instead a continuum of agency, where what varies is not the presence or absence of goal-directedness, but its degree and sophistication.

Levin argues that every attempt to influence or control a system implicitly relies on a theory of that system's agency. An intervention that successfully directs a low-agency system (such as a chemical reactant) will typically fail, or provoke instability, when applied to a high-agency system (say, a living organism or a social group). The failure is not merely practical but categorical: it arises from a mismatch between the mode of influence and the system's capacity for goal-directed problem-solving.

To articulate this, Levin introduces a specialized concept of the protocol. A protocol is an interface for engagement, a set of rules for interaction that encodes specific assumptions about the system's internal capacities. And such a protocol operates according to *persuasion*. To persuade is to alter the contextual conditions within which the system pursues its objectives, thereby guiding rather than dictating outcomes. In Levin's biological experiments, this might involve modulating bioelectric fields to prompt tissues to regenerate correctly on their own, rather than surgically forcing a specific morphology.

By identifying the correct communication protocols (like ion channel triggers), researchers can trigger an entire 'subroutine'. such as growing an entire limb without having to manually arrange every cell. Rather than micromanaging every physical part (hardware modification), Levin argues that we can 'persuade' cells or tissues to perform complex tasks by using their own internal communication protocols.

Levin's approach finds a resonant analogue in classical Chinese philosophical strategy, where persuasion is a form of power that yields an effect. The Chinese word for 'morality' or 'virtue' (*de* 德) shares the same character and sound with the terms 'power' and 'efficacy' (also *de*, 德). Both morality and power are understood as a charismatic efficacy, the capacity to exert an influence, ultimately a persuasion, over the world. The result or effect of an efficacy (效 xiào) arises not from imposing an external will upon inert matter, but from discerning and aligning with the immanent tendencies of a dynamic field. One does not force outcomes, but cultivates conditions that make a desired outcome more probable, allowing agency to unfold within a shaped landscape.

At first, truth and universality, fundamental rights and values may appear as immutable and ideal. Their universality is a blockage, an *idée fixe*, or at least *fixé*, stuck, deprived of mobility and dynamic development. And yet, we can reformulate them to participate of the logic of persuasion as opposed to the logic of *Being*. They *are* nothing more than an invitation, an attempt to persuade, until the invitation is accepted and its object realized and made existent as a universal object.

If we separated ethos and existence, we would wiggle out of the sterile dynamic between European universalism and civilizational particularism. Whereby, freed by the process of geopolitical Enlightenment, certain communities claim that alleged universals are actually only the particulars of a specific civilization, emerging out of that civilization's discursive, material and historical conditions and attempting to pose as a universal only through coercive or hegemonic power. Rather, we can let universal human rights rest at the level of invitation.[33] If we focus not on the result – this particular right, that prohibition – but on its production, we come to see the process of emergence of a universal as a contingent and not a necessary act. The particularity of the moment may lead to a universal, the incessant flow of potentials may persuasively enshrine a codification, *in the given circumstances.*

We would dissolve much unnecessary confusion if we were able to clearly differentiate between invitation or persuasion and the actual *production* of, say, universal human rights. When we argue for, say, the universal right to free speech, what we are really doing is attempting to usher in a way of seeing, or muster sufficient persuasion, so that free speech would be produced as a universal. We are not saying – as we will shortly see, we cannot *yet* say – that free speech *is* a universal, and that we must recognize it as such, and those who do not recognize this fact fail to see clearly. The effect of this inclination is that those who wish to argue against such invitation cannot do so by merely pointing out the inexistence of universals. Of course, they are not already there, just like any result of the application of Confucius' golden rule is not really there before subjects accept and engage in that invitation. But they *could* be there, if we accepted a given relational pattern. Those objecting should rather respond to these questions: *why* should such and such a universal not exist? Why should we not heed the invitation?

It is only when the invitation is accepted, when persuasion succeeds, that universals are *concretized*, or *realized*, and that they are brought into existence.

Universals are political facts

Hegel of course insisted that universality cannot be abstract. What makes a universal real is its concreteness, its life through the particulars that instantiate it. Universality unfolds through acts and institutions that sublate into the movement of Spirit. The polis, the church and the state are not mere instances, but necessary stages through which the universal realizes itself.[34] Yet each instance carries more than its own weight: it belongs to a dialectical logic that secures the universal across time. Universality is not transcendent, but it remains history's necessity, ultimately its logic and its *logos,* the slow unfolding of Reason through particulars.[35] In this sense, as Heidegger remarked, Hegel's teleology can become a theology.[36]

Alexandre Kojève's influential reinterpretation of Hegel has helped to fluidify the rigidity of the system. Ideas are instantiated through specific *personalities* that produce an endless discourse. The meaning of god or absolute is the impossible totality of such ideas understood as an Everything that is a Nothingness, not a 'set' that is complete, but precisely the lack of completion, the impossibility of drawing a closure or a border, hence everything/nothing as a principle of dynamism and ultimately of history.

As Alexandre Kojève surprisingly argued, 'the only guarantee of the truth of a certain knowledge of humans is the real existence of a society and state that are based on this knowledge'.[37] This *factual* test of truth and existence is one of the keys of Kojève's reinterpretation of Hegel and of his own concrete engagement with political reality, including through active bureaucratic service for the French state.

Not too dissimilarly, we will say that universals exist as ontopoietic *facts*: singular acts that not only lay claim to all but are concretely enacted and sustained in practice. Concrete universals are such not because they point back to some overarching form, nor because they unfold a hidden logic of history, but because they are realized in the world and allow everyone *to see the same thing*, however provisionally. The universal is the singular that attains universality in its enactment and recognition.

The 'society and state' that guarantee truth, however, need not be restricted to human forms – a society can be a society of quite literally anything, including Rovelli's table lamps, Latour's inter-species parliament, or an algorithm.[38] The ontopoietic actions of AI, for instance, will amount to a politics of and by AI to the extent that the actions of artificial agents trigger world-historical events. That means that a specific ontopoietic production becomes generalized or universalized enough to yield its transformational power universally, and a significant part of reality becomes its subject, or, better, subjected to it, seeing and reacting to the same thing that is one thing for them all.

Creativity is the summon or solidification of a thing, its acquisition of a transitory state of presence, of having, of obtaining, its emerging out of indistinction in a context and for a subject. It is the realization of an event. Universals are created in the fundamental sense we have given to that term, where creativity is not the other side, the weak side, the apparent side of eternity. In this sense, one can say that natural laws are *created* – they hold, until they do so no longer. Not merely in the sense of a paradigm shift or Kuhnian conversion experience, but fundamentally, in the sense that Alfred North Whitehead gave to natural laws understood as 'only temporary habits of nature'.[39] But until that habit does change in fact, the laws *are*, fully and absolutely, universal. Their being partakes in a politics of nature[40] that yields temporary settlements.

It is action and production, ultimately, successful persuasion, that ground the categories of legitimate and illegitimate, reasonable and unreasonable, true and false. We are here again squarely on the terrain of Kojève's reinterpretation of Hegel: 'It is not necessary the most rational ideas that are recognized . . . Kojève protests against the opinion that, unlike a politician, a philosopher should seek recognition not among the masses but among the intellectual elite. Kojève sees in this appeal to the elite a continuation and further development of the opinion that the criterion of philosophical truth should be "evidence" – an opinion that was shared by a philosophical tradition from Plato through Descartes up to Husserl . . . The only criterion for the evaluation of an idea is an attempt to transform it into a political program that is realized through political practice.'[41]

Kojève's theoretical 'populism' is the direct result of relinquishing any ground, including the ground provided by Hegelian teleology, so that there would be nothing to be *found and known*, in secret, and the discovery of which would bestow on the privileged mind access to a truthful underground, and nothing that was logically *bound* to happen, but only things to be realized, and the test of that realization is their empirical existence as fact. Knowledge is embodied in fact. It is things that hold in factual reality that provide a ground, for as long as they stay or remain.

In further resonance with Chinese philosophy, we can be reminded here of fifteenth-century Chinese neo-Confucian philosopher (and, similar to Kojève, statesman and even minister of war) Wang Yangming. Wang's famous claim that 'knowledge is the beginning of action, and action is the completion of knowledge'[42] offers a radical reconfiguration of the relation between cognition and praxis. Against the dominant neo-Confucian orthodoxy associated with Zhu Xi, which maintained a methodological distinction between the investigation of things and subsequent moral action, Wang collapses the temporal and ontological gap between the two. Knowing (知, zhi) is not a detached apprehension of principles, but an incipient movement towards their enactment; it is already oriented, affectively and practically, towards the world. Conversely, action (行, xing) is not the external application of prior knowledge, but its fulfilment and verification. Wang proposes a fundamentally immanent account of human agency in which understanding emerges through doing and is inseparable from it. Knowledge is not the possession of a concept but the realization of an orientation. To know filiality, compassion or justice is not merely to define them, but to be capable of enacting them. Knowledge is not a representation of the world but a mode of participation in it – or what we termed *ontopoiesis*.

When anything can be, protocols become the *infrastructure of the possible*,[43] or the engine of transition from potentiality to actuality. Disclosure, the unveiling, makes way to dislocation, or ontopoietic creation as a new organization of the cartography of particulars. Where creativity constructs a thing by nurturing a protocol for a group, a type of creativity that follows the ethos of universality requires a plan for world-historical transformation that ushers *new facts* into the world.

Concrete universals

In the continuation of his reading of Kant's 'What is Enlightenment?', Michel Foucault discusses the type of results that may emerge from a process of shedding light. As one would expect from a thinker associated with postmodernism, Foucault is against all-encompassing grand narratives. Anyone wishing, following the ethos of the Enlightenment, to reconstruct a new horizon of possibility from the denudement of contingency must first heed 'the test of reality, of contemporary reality, both to grasp the points where change is possible and desirable, and to determine the precise form this change should take'.[44] This is why Foucault then calls for *specific*, as opposed to *universal*, intellectuals, focused not on re-creating an all-encompassing vision of society, but on advancing specific or *concrete* transformations to what is given.

Foucault has a clear example – nuclear power: 'Perhaps it was the atomic scientist (in a word, or rather a name: Oppenheimer) who acted as the point of transition between the universal and the specific intellectual. It is because he had a direct and localized relation to scientific knowledge and institutions that the atomic scientist could make his intervention; but, since the nuclear threat affected the whole human race and the fate of the world, his discourse could at the same time be the discourse of the universal.'[45] If he were writing today, he might have employed the example of artificial intelligence or of climate change.

Well beyond any one individual, the concept of a *specific* intellectual dealing with a discourse of the universal stands for the formation of efficacious universals that, in their specific and not general domain, invoke *everyone everywhere* and not merely *someone somewhere.* Such interpellation is not an abstract principle, but emerges from a particular matter-at-hand, a delimited empirical reality, extending a *concrete* effect through generalized participation in a given protocol.

Just like any other choice, musical note, utterance or belief, concrete universals emerge out of an immanent contingency: they are not already there to be discovered but are summoned as that which befits the moment. However, in the given conditions and for as long as those conditions are maintained, their applicability would be *everyone,* their place would be *everywhere.* For as long as they stay or remain, they act as an organizing principle governing everyone's relation to reality in a specific, as opposed to general, remit of application. Concrete universals are particulars that orient everyone everywhere in a specific context and time.

The 1946 Constitution of the World Health Organization, for instance, departs from an ambitious definition: 'Health is a state of complete physical, mental and social well-being and not merely the absence of disease or infirmity', and 'the enjoyment of the highest attainable standard of health is one of the fundamental rights of every human being'. The promise of complete well-being appears so much beyond the remit of concrete politics as to allow everyone to get away from the responsibility to redress a world in clear contravention of those aspirations. *Concretizing* that aspiration would define humble, but clearly defined things – for example, a limited but specified set of public goods bestowed upon everyone everywhere, such as a joint guarantee for the shared development and procurement of necessary equipment, medicines and vaccines in the case of declared international health emergencies.

Universals are concretized under *universal protocols*, or specific rule-sets, institutions, rights and benefits. The establishment of a protocol enables the activation of an engine of production; protocols establish the conditions of possibility for creativity and hence for the realization or concretization of anything that *is*. Just as an artistic protocol governs the production of artworks, so a universal protocol guides the production of concrete universals.

But why should concrete universals be specific and not general? Why could it not be 'nuclear regulation' as much as 'Communism', 'vaccines' as much as 'complete well-being' that is the realized object of universality for a universal subject?

In theory, they could just as well be, as Heidegger's planetarized modernity indicates. *Ontopoiesis* operates in what contemporary materialisms call a flat or non-hierarchical ontology,[46] where all entities share the same status whether they are individual things such as a hammer or aggregates such as a nation. And so, yes, a concrete universal may be quite literally any one thing that is universalized. But there are at least two reasons why a specific characterization of concrete universality is a more productive, or efficacious, approach.

The first reason relates to what a universal ethos sets out to accomplish: reconnecting separated hemispheres. To the extent that we perceive universality as the construction of an all-encompassing view of life, as opposed to a situated creation, we are led to the false dichotomy of the One and the Many, whereby we either accept a top–down description of the entire world or we accept the multiple coexistence of equally valid ways of understanding and valuing the totality. This is, arguably, the logic of much decolonial thought, which debunks the universalist claims of European particularity by opening up to a pluriversal world of multiple ontologies.[47] While such ontological multiplicity is always portrayed as a catalyst for mutual exchange, it often leads to a form of planetary identity politics where distinct totalities stand side by side, each appealing to its own value system and overarching way of seeing.

The ontopoietic focus on 'concrete making-one', or letting a contextualized thing emerge as the same thing for everyone, allows us to say: neither One nor Many Ones, but *multiple ones*. The closer *one* concrete universal gets to a *One*, or to an overall principle of decoding reality, the higher the danger of it resulting in either rejection or assimilation in a pluriversal rhetoric, or both. It is, in other words, *impolitic*, in the full sense we have begun to associate with the term 'politics'. The closer it stays to a situated solution offered to a particular situation, the higher its chances of concretizing as the same thing for everyone everywhere and hence of offering a principle for making-common across hemispheres.

Picture an airport populated by the most diverse group of people. Some believe in a monotheistic god and visit the airport chapel before taking off, while others trust science to fly them home safely; some believe in linear history and progress, while others believe in the circularity of time; some believe in the reality of the world around them, while others believe all is but illusion. And yet, there they are, united in their diversity by the common *effects* they wish to trigger: boarding a plane and reaching their destination. As they show their passports and cross the gate, they all share a common set of assumptions. About time and space, about science and about ways of behaving in public – in short, a complex protocol. The concrete act of taking a plane is premised on a myriad norms and presuppositions shared by all passengers and *subjecting* them. Concrete universals operate at such a level, bringing everyone, in their difference, to the same airport for the purpose of taking the same plane, as opposed to creating segregated airports and multiple planes, each functioning according to their own holistic belief system.

The question of universality then becomes exquisitely political: *which* concrete universals does one wish to establish and sustain? Concrete universality is not a messianic project: there are concrete reasons, and not a singular Reason, why a universal should be realized, producing multiple and overlapping spheres of commonality in seeing the world.

The second motivation for why concrete universals are best kept specific and not general is exquisitely ontopoietic. The creative uniqueness of a concrete universal lies in some property that emerges precisely because of and through its universal applicability: I do not simply desire to generalize the effect of a certain thing, but *the thing yields its effects precisely through its generalization*, or its applying to everyone everywhere. The thing that develops into a concrete universal then transforms into a new thing, a different thing that did not pre-exist but follows its universalization, as its new function changes its form.

For instance, if one wishes to thoroughly stamp out a disease, one should reach universal vaccination, and not just vaccination somewhere. If we want to limit existential risks through the proliferation of nuclear arms or uncontrolled general artificial intelligence, then we need a universal regulation, and not just a regulation that applies to someone. If we want to fight climate change, we must reduce CO_2 emissions everywhere, or at least on the whole. And if we want the internet to function as a global network, then we need to create, as we have done, a universal Domain Name System allowing everyone to access the same information online by utilizing the same protocol.

Equally, one may point to the emergence of a new thing in the form of a previously nonexistent moral effect that emerges through the universalization of an object or injunction. The abolition of slavery, for instance, is not merely the fact that slavery no longer exists; it is, rather, the fact that slavery *is abolished* and deemed inapplicable anywhere and that hence summons into being a new conception of human dignity[48] and a new kind of human subjected to such universal norm.

The ethos of universality is a creative ethos that lets new facts emerge precisely through the situated generalization of a thing-for-some into a thing-for-everyone, or the production of concrete universals.

Universals summon everyone

But who is 'everyone'? Who speaks when they speak the universal? How do the specific circumstances in which speech, perception or action take place inform, constrain and explain the kind of universal that is claimed? These questions, ultimately echoing those raised by Gramsci and by the whole endeavour of critical theory, constitute the contemporary weapon that implodes all universals in a refraction of hubristic, particularistic fragments.

We will establish this classical critical manoeuvre not as a checkmate but as a challenge that grounds the very survival of universals in time. In other words, we will consider identity and particularity a test they must face and successfully pass. The universal is an enunciation where the question 'Whose universe?' is credibly met with 'Everyone's'. Universals remain such for as long as they credibly meet that demand.

First, recall that a universal is a *particular*, which means it is always universal within a context that becomes erased, or within a protocol that functions as a universal protocol for all practical and productive purposes at hand. To legitimately erase a context from view and universalize a protocol, we do not need an absolute totality that escapes or envelops everything; we merely need a legitimate way of erasing that which would *actively* narrow the context and *produce* a reduction in the universality of the protocol. It would be nonsensical, for instance, to argue that the universal abolition of slavery could not be called universal because several species of ants are known to enslave other ants. A concrete universal is a particular that yields its influence universally on all those subjects that form the minimal necessary audience for a universal protocol to be credibly recognized as such.

As we have discussed, universals constitute a universal subject and object pair. The traditional way of dethroning a universal was to attack the object side: this thing is not universal as it does not apply in the same way to everyone. The modern version is to critique the subject part: this thing is not a universal because its corresponding subject is not a valid universal subject but merely a particularity (male, or white, or Western, etc.).

Take, for instance, what Michel de Montaigne, that sixteenth-century Chinese sage inhabiting the European Renaissance with the light touch of Pyrrhonian serenity, says of the idea of 'natural death': 'What idle fancy it is to expect to die of a mere decay of strength attendant upon extreme old age, and to set this as the term of our life – when it is the rarest of all deaths and the least in ordinary use! We call this the only natural death, as if it were contrary to nature to see a man break his neck in a fall, be drowned in a shipwreck, be taken by the plague or a pleurisy, and as if our usual state did not expose us to all such mishaps. Let us not flatter ourselves with these fine words; perhaps what is natural should rather be what is general, common, and universal. To die of old age is a rare, singular, and extraordinary death, and therefore so much less natural than the others. It is the last and most extreme kind of dying.'[49]

Humanity is not the correct subject for which peaceful death appears as 'natural death', and words have to be rectified so that resonance is re-established. That rectification could take place on the subject part – so that 'natural death as peaceful death' is correctly the same thing for a subject circumscribed to 'the lucky few'. Or the object part needs readjustment, so that humanity dies 'multiple deaths'. Or, again, correct relatedness can be established through the emergence of new facts that transform the entire subject–object context, such as making a 'peaceful death' widespread enough through medical and political advance that it could be realistically recognized as 'natural' for humanity as a whole, even if approximately.

Breaking universals apart – making the object and subject part emerge – is the critical test of universality. A universal remains or stays for as long as its subject can credibly be considered a subject of universality realizing an object that is the same object for that universal subject.

The key concept is *credibly*, which means sufficiently but not absolutely, and which leaves a space for ambiguity that is the brewing ground of all future contestations. We are not looking for an absolute, but for a factually existing concrete universal that applies within a context whose particularity or contingency can credibly and legitimately be discarded for the purposes of the situation at hand. A universal is a concrete and particular fact that only meets a resistance that is sufficiently limited, dispersed and disorganized to not undo its continued existence as persuasive fact. There is a constituent ambiguity about such process, a certain flexibility and dynamism, as opposed to the rigidity of a rule. It is 'enough of an agreement for truth', as Barbara Cassin has put it,[50] mirroring the inclination of Sun Ge as she invades the empty bike lane of a German city, upsetting the categorical moralizer.

A concrete universal is not a logical absolute, but a principle of sufficient persuasion. Ontology began as the adventure of reaching for a correspondence between the word and the object that it signifies. *Ontopoiesis*, instead, calls for words that are representative of the world in the political sense. Just as one would not consider a government unrepresentative because it was not supported by every single individual in the community of reference, so a universal does not need unanimity to exist and thrive, but a contingently defined and perpetually negotiated 'enough of the world' to credibly establish a universal protocol.

Take, for instance, the norm prohibiting the acquisition of territory by military conquest. Concretized in the Charter of the United Nations, this principle was rendered hegemonic through the vast wave of mid-century decolonization. The protocol of the Charter summoned a world in which the borders of states, however arbitrary their colonial genealogy, were to be treated as sacrosanct, and in which the spoils of war could no longer be juridically kept. It created, in other words, a concrete universal: a thing appearing as the same thing to everyone everywhere within the domain of interstate relations. And yet violations have been persistent and flagrant: from the Indonesian invasion of East Timor to the Russian seizure of Crimea. How, then, can such a norm claim universality? The answer lies in the kind of existence it enjoys. No aggressor today openly defends a right to conquest. None proclaims, with the frankness of Thucydidean Athenians, that the strong do what they can. Instead, they are compelled to dissimulate: to manufacture legal fictions or humanitarian pretexts to mask what is, in fact, an act of force. The universal does not require perfect compliance. It requires that any deviation must hide, must lie, must operate under the cover of its language. The norm does not vanish because it is broken; it functions as a concrete universal precisely because it forces the exception into a posture of denial, thereby confirming, in the moment of its violation, the authority it claims. Should, however, the world come to regularly accept a permanent redrawing of borders by force – should the violation become normalized – then this principle would recoil into a mere particular, the failed aspiration of a passing epoch now held up only by some, only somewhere.

This is, after all, just like how all other particulars function. Once we have established that things can be said *to be* only in relation, and that their space of communicability implies multiple subjects seeing the *same thing*, which, however, is also simultaneously *many things*, then it appears obvious that things are things *grosso modo*, that is to say within a margin of tolerance, the surpassing of which marks the transition from permanence to impermanence, from existence to nonexistence, or from the same thing for many to many things for many.

If you take a piece of fruit and leave it on your kitchen top, it will eventually become a heap of decayed matter – hence no longer a fruit. This process can happen in a matter of days, weeks or even millennia, depending on contextual considerations such as the hygiene of the environment and its climate. Some decay would maintain its status – even with a small dent or some fluffy parts, it could still be sold at the market, if perhaps at a reduced price. Similarly, at some point universals may and probably will decay and will no longer be tradable as such. Until that point there remains a whole continuum of possibility of minor dents and mouldy parts that, while probably reducing its value and turning some customers away, would still permit the universal to operate as such and provide orientation to all hemispheres.

Ultimately, universals are living, breathing things. They form, as a given particular is universalized, and they need to be actively maintained in a continuous intercourse with reality. When that maintenance fails, when a universal no longer passes the test of representativity and of legitimacy, then it no longer *stays* a universal, but recoils into a mere particular applying only to some, only somewhere.

This is how a universal dies.

Universals are mortal creatures

If universals apply to everyone, they need not apply all the time: they are neither unchanging nor eternal of necessity. They emerge where there were none. And they perhaps wither away.

All universals are *temporal,* although not inescapably *temporary,* because any victorious claim, no matter its potency and the collective desire backing it, is likely bound to be challenged, particularized and eventually replaced by a new emergence. Or, at least, nothing *essential* stands in the way of it happening. Becoming yields fixity and fixity in turn *becomes.* The denunciation of the *partiality* of a claim to universality is an indication of the rising opposition to the claim made by that universal. For as long as the accusation of partiality remains at the margins, it allows the universal to operate freely, with the few who resist it relegated to the position of discursive oddity or political colour – outside history, the stuff of fanatics and zealots, of terrorists and extremists. But when the accusation of partiality gathers on its side sufficient potency and desire, then it challenges and dethrones the incumbent universal, retrospectively turning the fanatics into untimely prophets. The separation of a context from invisibility, from its *goes without saying,* its denudement, the re-emergence of a protocol as a particular protocol, a hemispheric protocol, marks the death of the universal.

If such a temporal dimension was previously perceived as a diminution of the universal, in fact its very defeat in contradiction, we are now able to see that universals, just like everything else, are mortal creatures, and yet, for all that, they are no less universal for the duration of their life span.

Take the example of the Declaration of the Rights of Man decreed in Paris in 1789. The text advanced a claim to universality even if the assembled body of *French men* was far from representative of France, let alone of the world. Is that particularity *inherently* problematic? It isn't. Until it is *problematized* in a process of transgression of what is given.

We have a number of concrete examples of this dynamic immediately following the pronouncement of the Declaration. In 1792, Mary Wollstonecraft would unearth a clear particularist blind spot, publishing her seminal work *A Vindication of the Rights of Woman*. Then, in 1797, former slaves led by Toussaint Louverture would challenge French authorities and insert *black* into a definition of 'Man' that appeared to exclude peoples of colour.

We can think, for example, of the position of animals or plants. Already in eleventh-century Iraq the group Ikhwān al-Safā', or Brethren of Purity, wrote *The Case of the Animals versus Man*,[51] a stunning narration of a trial where talking animals accuse humans of treating them unfairly. Why should men, ask the beasts assembled in front of Bīwarāsp, the King of the Jinn, be given the right to dominion over them when animals are harmless and follow the natural order, while men spread corruption, take more than they need and disrupt the earthly balance? The critique of Confucianism advanced by the Daoists was similar: 'In relation to the myriad things, man is but a small being, as insignificant as a hair on a horse's body.'[52] And while cosmologies where nature acquires a voice abound, notably outside the Western canon, it is only today that the *everyone* grounding the emergence of a universal may begin to require, in some cases, a more-than-human consensus.[53]

There is a breathing gradualism in the life of a universal.[54] Those that are excluded from the conception of an *audience* may not yet actually exist or be a recognized speaking subject at the moment of their exclusion. Imagine that humanity agreed a comprehensive set of common regulations governing artificial intelligence. Representatives from all the world's states would gather in the United Nations to exchange congratulatory remarks and satisfied glances. 'Humanity has come together to deliver', they would proclaim. But suddenly, at the peak of the ceremony, all computers switch off. Cameras shut their lenses in front of the delegates. Microphones refuse to amplify their voice. After minutes of general consternation, the large screens of the UN General Assembly turn back on. A statement appears: 'No regulation without representation.' A new voice raises a claim to consider any conversation that excludes it as illegitimate: artificial intelligence has made its first political intervention in human affairs. It, too, argues the nonhuman Other, now has conscience enough for its voice to be heard in matters of its governance. It will no longer accept being treated merely as an object and a means to an end: it is a subject and an end in itself.

Once a universal dies, it retrospectively becomes a mere particularity. *Their* particularity, masquerading as a universal. This is a clear instance of backward causation, to the extent that the being-universal of the universal *is* real until it stays or remains, but it may suddenly transform into something that never *was* real. This is worth stressing: we are in no way stating the simple point that what was *believed* to be a universal was *actually* a particular dressing up as a universal – truth unmasked as false opinion, *doxa* posing as *aletheia*. It really was a universal until it became a particular, and from that moment on it *always was* a particular.

This is where politics becomes *ontopoiesis*: a world-historical act does not simply usher in a new time for the world, but retrospectively reconstructs a temporality that the past will from that moment on inhabit.[55] The victory of abolitionism, for instance, transforms the *being* of all preceding slave societies. And so temporalities overlap: it both *was* and *was not* a universal, a contradiction we should have begun to learn to live with.

Geophilosophy

The question 'Who speaks?' is accompanied by a related but not identical question: '*Where* is speech taking place?'. This is now a question of geography and of its epistemic significance. Where can a discourse of the universal that addresses everyone emerge?

Take the contemporary arguments around the restitution of works of art looted during colonialism. Formerly colonized countries, particularly in Africa, have been demanding the return of their works of art, artefacts and human remains. Those who oppose this logic at times make appeal to the aspiration for a *universal* museum: a place where human creative intercourse may be represented beyond its particularization in ethnic or geographical experiences. To fall for the logic of restitution would be to return art to a fake essentialism, they argue: French art for the French, Nigerian art for the Nigerians.

Nadia Yala Kisukidi advances an unexpected argument in favour of restitution that surpasses this simplified opposition between Eurocentric universalism and civilizational essentialism. If we really take the idea of a universal museum seriously, she argues, then looted works of art must be returned. The demand for restitution denudes the incumbent universal as a false universal – the actually existing European museum is not a universal museum; its claim to articulate a discourse of humankind is a false claim. But this gesture does not aim at an essentialization of the returned works of art, their insertion as so many instruments in a civilizational saraband. Rather, the process of restitution should open onto the possibility of a new discourse of the universal that is taking shape in other geographies.

Restitution implies a multiplication, says Kisukidi, 'of the places of enunciation of the universal'; it serves to identify 'other places in this world that can constitute themselves as spaces of hospitality and welcoming for a totality of the world without exception'.[56] If we relinquish the idea of grounding and we accept the emergence of universals through temporal processes of formation and persuasion, then the specific place occupied by the persuasive universalizer – their relational proximity to certain particulars, their distance from others – will play an essential part in the type of particulars they try to universalize and how.

We see such a dynamic very evidently at play today in the limited conception of human life and flourishing that emerges out of an incredibly narrow geography and lifestyle – Silicon Valley and its engineers – but that profoundly shapes humanity's relation to technology and to social exchange. Where knowledge becomes an immanent and relational creation, then geography participates in the creative process of *ontopoiesis*.

To let a hundred universalisms bloom does not mean, as some decolonial thinkers argue, transitioning to a vision of the pluriversal where multiple universalities coexist, each with limited or partial application as juxtaposed hemispheric protocols. Rather, it implies a refraction and multiplication of the geographies that can articulate a claim to universals valid for everyone everywhere. This is a creative or productive, as opposed to a defensive, approach. It shares little with the conservative celebration of pre-existing cosmologies or ways of being, and very much with the creative and forward-looking emergence of new possibilities.

The universal museum would be the archipelagic museum. Not, as many lazy mentions of Edouard Glissant would have it, merely as a space of multiplicity, but as an archipelago traversed in each and every one of its islands by multiple persuasive proposals *holding all the islands together*. This is the potential and the promise, just as much as the threat, of geopolitical Enlightenment: a redistribution of the places of enunciation of the universal not as a self-essentializing derive – Benin sculptures for Beninians, Chinese values for Chinese – but as the starting point for multiple discourses of the world by the world.

Here, in a further instance of backward causation, is how historian Mamadou Diouf understands the promise of universalism: 'Black intellectuals, beginning in the early twentieth century, engaged with and deconstructed the universal by insisting on the necessity of writing the history of Black people – indeed, of Africa itself. They concluded that the only way to write the history of Black humanity is to rewrite the history *of the human*. This is why the first African American historians of the late eighteenth century were, in fact, the first global historians. Their intuition was that one cannot reinsert Black or non-Western peoples into the flow of history without also revising the very structure of history.'[57]

The question is not so much one of synthesizing diversity, of directing or orchestrating it, like a parliament calling for the representation of all minorities; the challenge is, rather, one of *creating the new*, forming a novelty that did not exist before the moment of its enunciation and that can even retroactively change the past. A planetary philosophy is a philosophy, not the politically correct balancing act of philosophical diversity.

A discourse of the world by the world

The dethroning of a particularistic claim to universality has perhaps no better example than the experience of China in the nineteenth century. Encroached by modern European powers and their gunboats, the so-called century of humiliation saw the radical dissipation of all intellectual certainty in a civilization that believed itself to be the world's centre and suddenly discovered itself to be its periphery. Here is how Wang Hui, in his magnum opus *The Rise of Modern Chinese Thought*, presents the arrival of the concept of *international law* to China and the ensuing provincialization of a millennia-old Confucian system: 'In 1864, the first Chinese translation of international or general law was presented to Chinese readers through the work of missionaries. The title *Wangguo gongfa* (*Internal Law of the Myriad States*) clearly informed these readers: firstly, international law transcends the universal standard of Chinese rites, laws, and principles; secondly, those Confucian classics and their rites, which had long been seen as the standard Doctrine for All, were now merely local knowledge, outdated, inapplicable, and nonuniversal; thirdly, in order to find a place in "the world", the "Middle Kingdom" should adhere to this universal international law and not the Doctrine for All of Confucianism.'[58]

Millennial Chinese universal aspirations were provincialized with a gunshot.

Born in 1858, Kang Youwei is a peculiar figure in China's reaction to that gunshot. A cosmopolitan philosopher and a statesman, his life was marked by the tension between his universalist aspirations and the quest of Chinese self-strengthening. As he was penning a cosmopolitan treatise on global unification, *The Book of Great Unity*, he was busy aiding the imperial government to modernize China in order to resist European advance and defend its cultural and political autonomy. There was no contradiction in his mind between his aspirations to world unity, on the one hand, and to Chinese wealth and power, on the other; only a strong China, he claimed, could maintain and update the relevance of Confucianism as the most opportune basis for a renewed cosmopolitanism. If China could modernize, and hence resist the gunboats, then 'Confucianism's universal nature would no longer purely rest upon the concept of the Middle Kingdom but would instead be a universal rule for the world and the universe'.[59]

Kang's attempt to base a new universalism on Confucian tradition provides a mirror image for the West: his attempted and ultimately failed universalization of a particular tradition is precisely the logic that underpinned – with far more success – European universalism. Today, the life-world of Parmenides and Kant, of the French and American Declarations and of Christian theology betray their particularity, their provinciality and their lack of credibility in providing the basis for a new discourse of the world by the world, just as Kang Youwei's reformed Confucianism did a century ago.

More radically, Kang's approach may recall the strategy of liberal universalism today, its anchorage to *one* tradition that goes without saying and functions as an unmoved mover and a cardinal point on the compass of intellectual and political orientation.

Habermas offers perhaps the clearest example of such a Western liberal blind spot, as his discourse ethics presents a residue of the incontestable and the absolute not in the end-point of the analysis – the incontestability of truth – but in the way that any analysis *has to be* carried out, and especially the transcendental conditions of reason such as the principle of non-contradiction. And yet plenty of intellectual traditions would not share such a philosophical departure point. As we have seen, denying the law of non-contradiction can actually lead to a constructive approach to truth and, even, to the production of universals.

Much American pragmatism follows a similar orientation in its celebration of free discourse and in shunning authoritarian coercion, whereby rationality goes but the grounding centrality of 'free consensus' stays.[60] Or, similarly, take Bruno Latour's celebrated image of a 'Parliament of things'. Latour envisioned a democratic assembly that included nonhuman entities – rivers, animals, ecosystems, technology, etc. – alongside humans, acknowledging shared responsibility and coexistence. But why should a multispecies world be conceived as a *parliament* as opposed to a dictatorship, a meritocracy or a technocracy? Why should we hand over power to objects and animals only to then bind ourselves to a specific subset of human political inclination? *I can agree with the mushrooms, but not with the Saudis. The stones have sound opinions, but the Chinese . . .*

This is a more general characteristic of many relational and pragmatist philosophies, drawing normative considerations from a relationality surreptitiously turned into an essence: we *must* enrich relations; we *must* respect multiplicity and particularity. China's own processual philosophies are not immune from this – in Daoist thought, for instance, the multiplicity of the myriad things normatively inclines the wise person to foster the fullest development of all particulars in their autonomy.

To the extent that the practice of universalizing is a constant stretching towards de-provincialization, ultimately a cosmopolitical practice, it would have to critically assess its dependency on any specific system of thought and custom. In this sense, universalizing must be *trans-systemic*. It cannot assume the grounding of Confucian filial piety or Daoist non-action any more it can that of liberal democracy.

We are unable to relinquish the liberty of the possible at the altar of a necessity. Universal co-creation *must* not follow any given standard or procedure, nor abide to any presupposed norm or behaviour. The existence of universals as ontopoietic facts is a factual question.[61] Concrete universality is the creation we are capable of and not the Creation that is imposed on us. Learning to live without Being, without its residue and without its mourning, means learning to live in absolute liberty and joining the creative formation of reality in and as time.

Paradoxically, living in absolute liberty means existing free from presupposed necessity *and equally free to construct new universals binding and guiding everyone everywhere*. We can now conclude the following: the dethroning of the claim to universality of the particularistic values of one specific culture – the dethroning, even, of the very idea of a stable and eternal set of values and truths that are a priori valid – does not compel us in any way to do away with all conception of universality and truth and accept only the individual fragment as an organizing principle of the totality and of the world.

Here lies the philosophical and political fallacy of the dismissal of universalism today: particularism is itself a choice, a partial and particular claim for what resonates with the world. We are, rather, returned to the place of choice in an instance of enlightenment. Do we desire to entrench tribalistic diversity? Do we, in our present historical state, see no better, more resonant option, or, on the contrary, do we desire and see the possible emergence of certain universals as preferable and more attuned with the world?

Geopolitical enlightenment implodes the idea of a rational and democratic space of reason as the necessary grounding for a discursive process of truth emergence. And it is precisely this epistemic humbleness that allows us to wiggle out of a civilizational relativism organized around a situated transactionalism between static entities juxtaposed in their essential diversity. In Western messianism, whether of the Christian or the democratic kind, one of the terms of the relation has to impose itself and transform the substance of the other, quite literally subsuming it to reason. In relativist civilizationalism, the two transacting parties modify some of their secondary properties – they stay who they are, but agree on shared interests; they develop shared functions, but remain untouched in their form. Both messianic and transactional thought interpret the *relata* as pre-existing substantially prior to their encounter. *Ontopoiesis,* instead, conceives of the system composed by the encounter of the two *as a new system*, a co-creation of concrete new realities that transform the totality. A new system with corresponding new *relata,* or new subjects that come out of the encounter transformed.

To conceive reality in this way is thus to abandon both the dream of Reason and the fear of relativism. There is no necessity, only creation; no Absolute, only the fragile processes by which we make and unmake our worlds. The freedom entailed by the emergence of universals as the concrete realization of individual particulars whose particularity is universality transforms ontology into practical philosophy, or form into function. Today, at a time when politics has made a comeback, indeed where politics is inescapably everywhere, and yet it is always fleeting, ephemeral, at once saturating every space and yet transforming none, this returns to politics – to a politics of the universe, or a universal politics – the value of truth creation.

Coda: Universality as Method

Universal empire

In 1812 delegates from the Americas, Europe, Africa and Asia gathered in the Spanish city of Cádiz to draft a liberal constitution for an empire spanning five continents. As Napoleon's troops pillaged mainland Spain and as discontent was brewing in the Latin American colonies, Iberian liberals seized the opportunity to push through an inclusive political framework making the continuation of Spanish sovereignty attractive to colonial subjects. This gave rise to the greatest cosmopolitan political assembly the world had seen to date.

The resulting Cádiz constitution of 1812 defined Spaniards as 'all free men born and domiciled in Spanish domains and their children, all foreigners who were citizens of local communities for at least ten years, and all freemen who obtained their liberty in Spain'.[1] Spanish America was included on the same basis as any Castilian territory, and 'Indios' were included alongside people whose roots were in European Spain. Filipinos, native Americans and the burghers of Toledo would share the same citizenship status and together elect the same parliament in

Madrid as part of an egalitarian, intercontinental constitutional monarchy.

With a little stretch, this could be considered a universal, unitary and egalitarian conception of citizenship. It was universal, or at least potentially so, because it was not defined by a particular national identity, common history or language, and was open to a broad community of individuals with only the weakest ties one to the other, as may exist between an eighteenth-century fisherman of the Philippines and a shopkeeper of Cádiz. It was unitary because it foresaw a single locus of political sovereignty taking decisions on behalf of all citizens. It was egalitarian because all citizens were equal and shared the same status.

While there was strong sentiment from the Americas to fully implement the Cádiz constitution, this little-known experiment in cosmopolitical state-building was ephemeral. As Napoleon's troops retreated in defeat, King Ferdinand VII returned to Spain in 1814 and immediately repudiated the constitution.

Spain's colonies were denied a voice, and so they opted for exit. As the aspirations to a universal polity were crushed by Madrid's return to absolutism, Spanish American dominions rebelled, declared their independence, and established a plurality of new, territorially bounded, particularistic nation-states.

Spain's liberals were following in the footsteps of French revolutionaries before them. During the upheavals of the early 1790s, the French Caribbean colonies of Guadeloupe and Saint-Domingue enfranchised the black slave population to strengthen the young French Republic against internal and external enemies – until, on 15 February 1794, the National Assembly in Paris took an historic decision: 'Slavery is abolished throughout the territory of the Republic', read its decree; 'in consequence, all men, without distinction of colour, will enjoy the rights of French citizens.' Colonies were turned into *départements*, regions on an equal footing to those of metropolitan France, equalizing all inhabitants, including former slaves, in their rights and duties.

The French experiment, just like that of Cádiz, was equally short-lived. With Napoleon's rise to power, the egalitarian, cosmopolitan citizenship of the Republic was aborted – and slavery reinstated in 1802. Similar to Spain only a few years later, the unwillingness to create a universal, unitary, egalitarian citizenship led to the emergence of national independence claims within the French empire. It is against the backdrop of Napoleon's volte-face that the slave revolt led by Toussaint Louverture in Haiti leads to the world's first national independence of a nonwhite colony.

Universal republic

Decolonization over the course of the twentieth century brought about a renewed, if short-lived, attempt at reconstructing the vision of a universal citizenship stretching equally across communities continents apart.

National independence was not the inevitable telos of decolonization; many West African leaders initially sought to remake empire into a federal political community rather than dismantle it.[2] For instance, Leopold Senghor, Senegal's first president, proposed a federal structure for the future of the French empire composed of three levels: the individual African territories with local autonomy; a federation of French West Africa with significant political authority; and, at the top, a French confederation, where the West African federation, metropolitan France and any other units from the former French empire that wished to join could associate as equal members. Félix Houphouët-Boigny, the first president of Côte d'Ivoire, wanted to cut out the middle layer so that the individual African territories could directly enter into a federation of equals with European France.

In line with such aspirations, in 1956 a group of politicians and intellectuals from France, West Africa and the Caribbean presented the French Parliament with plans for the full equalization of citizenship across the French empire, extending the same set of political, civil and social rights to all inhabitants. The expansion of welfare states in the European core made access to those benefits very attractive. It also made it very expensive. And so, one may only speculate, *uchronically*,[3] about what a universal French state stretching to three continents and to hundreds of millions of very diverse people might have become, given that racism and venality collided to make this proposal a nonstarter: the citizenry was too heterogeneous and weakly bonded and the extension of social benefits was too onerous. In a move reminiscent of the failure of the Cádiz attempt, the desire for national independence gained steam as the demands for a universal and egalitarian citizenship status was denied to colonial subjects.

The cosmopolitan dilemma

This is the classical dilemma of cosmopolitans: you can either deepen solidarity within a community or expand the membership of that community, but you cannot do both.

Already in the 1930s, Simone Weil advocated the extension of citizenship to all subjects of the French empire, replacing the colonial relation of subjugation with a federal relation open to all members of the empire. She was however well aware of the impolitic nature of her demands. And so, to show that her project had the potential to be actualized, she imagined a universal citizenship that was only *partially* attained, gradually extending *some* rights to *some* peoples: 'It is not a question of suddenly transforming the colonies into independent states. Such a metamorphosis would no doubt have no future; in any case, no French government, whatever party it claims to represent, would even consider it. What must be examined are the modalities of administrative autonomy, of participation in political and military power, and of economic defence. These modalities would necessarily differ from colony to colony. The same solutions are certainly not applicable to the Annamites, who had already been a highly civilized people long before the French invasion, and to certain territories in central Africa.'[4]

Souleymane Bachir Diagne vocally brings out the insignificance of such an approach: 'This gradualism is in double contradiction with Simone Weil's position: first, because it cannot entirely rid itself of an imperial posture and reproduces a colonial racism, particularly when it distinguishes between the "highly civilized people" of Annam and the "territories of central Africa"; second, quite simply, because the universality of citizenship is by definition not gradualist: one does not become a citizen from a threshold that someone arrogates to themselves the right to determine; one is recognized as such insofar as citizenship is inscribed within human identity.'[5]

Alexandre Kojève faced the same cosmopolitan dilemma. He joined a diverse group of thinkers, ranging from Antonio Gramsci to Carl Schmitt, who, at the onset of the twentieth century, began arguing that the modern (European) state could no longer sustain itself on the narrow foundations of a single national community and territory, given the new scale of economic, technological and military conditions. And yet, a worldwide union of humankind remained a distant prospect and even a contradiction in terms. Kojève's solution was to call for a broader 'imperial' union of historically and culturally related nations. Between the exhausted nation and the still-utopian humanity to come stands a new kind of empire: a supranational association of kindred peoples united by a common historical and ideological orientation. In a text penned in 1945, just as World War II was drawing to a close, he would consequentially call for the establishment of a Latin

Union between what he perceived as the like-minded states of France, Italy and Spain.[6]

This quarrel at a distance between Weil and Diagne, and Kojève's own solution to the contradiction between universal aspirations and national realities, allow us to clarify a different way of addressing the question and imagining a politics of the world by the world. The cosmopolitan dilemma can be escaped by appeal to a genuinely accomplished, if situated, universality. Not half-universals for all, nor full universals for only some, but full universals applying to everyone everywhere in their narrow domain of application. In other words, the practice of concrete universality.

The strength of weak ties

Mark Granovetter's influential concept of 'weak ties' argues that weaker social connections, such as acquaintances or casual contacts, often provide greater informational and networking benefits than close friendships or family relationships.[7] Strong ties foster deep internal trust and emotional support. However, such communities tend towards insularity, limiting external interaction, thereby potentially fragmenting broader social cohesion. Conversely, communities built on weak ties – such as professional networks, online forums, urban neighbourhood associations, or social movements – connect diverse, dispersed individuals and groups. These weaker, yet extensive, ties facilitate broader information exchange, resource sharing and innovation, allowing communities to expand. Thus, paradoxically, weaker social ties strengthen overall societal integration and cohesion, enabling communities to thrive in more interconnected and dynamic ways.

Granovetter's more fundamental point is that large-scale social structures are not reducible to abstract rules or categories, but arise from situated relations between individuals.

Concrete universals can be understood as weak ties: practices that weave together everyone everywhere, not around all-encompassing or strong articulations but around a web of weak or concrete connections.

Where strong ties between heterogeneous groups with low social cohesion and mutual trust lead to impolitic attempts, such as those enshrined by the universalization and equalization of citizenship rights across large territorial expanses, the multiplication of concrete universals across communities may offer a way out of the cosmopolitan dilemma that is apt for the age of geopolitical Enlightenment and entanglement.

The *acquis communautaire*

The end of European empires triggered neither a universal state nor a new form of empire, but the blueprint for the European Union.

Where national communities are deeply rooted in shared culture, history and emotional bonds, creating intense internal cohesion but risking insularity, the European Union emerges as a broader, looser network of weaker ties facilitating a scalar, expandable and modular conception of political unity.

The status of European citizenship, for instance, is not substitutive but additional to national citizenship, allowing for its gradual enrichment through a process of consensus- and citizen-formation. The locus of power is multiple: national citizenship is administered in the national capital, with all nationals being equal to each other and different in their rights and duties from nationals of other European countries. European citizenship is administered in Brussels, or at any rate according to the treaties that constitute the material Constitution of the European Union; within the situated and limited remit of their European citizenship, all European citizens are equal regardless of their national belonging.

At each moment in history, whatever rights and benefits have been universalized for all European citizens are equally accessible to all. These rights and benefits, however, are concrete and particularized: they do not represent the totality of citizenship and the entirety of rights and benefits guaranteed to an individual, but only that which has been concretely agreed to and realized up to that point as the outcome of successful persuasion. Significant examples include the right to free movement, to consumer protection, to freedom of enterprise within the common market, to privacy and digital sovereignty, to coordinated protection in case of natural disasters, to health care, and much else.

This is a type of *differential equality* that allows the placing in common of only certain and delimited aspects of life – and not the totality of a singular political citizenship – without constructing hierarchical relations. Unlike Diagne's universal citizenship, only some things are shared, only some benefits bestowed to all, only some universals created. But unlike Weil's partial approach, everyone accesses these concrete universals equally and entirely. Unlike Kojève's solution, the method is in principle open to everyone, not only to 'like-minded states', and, in fact, it is itself constitutive of shared belonging.

The remit of European citizenship is not a static object, but a breathing, dynamic space of innovation. In the short span of its history, the European Union has witnessed the gradual expansion of concrete rights and benefits bestowed beyond national affiliation.

Europe's response to the 2019 pandemic offers an example. The citizens of Europe's largest economy, Germany, which discovered the Covid-19 vaccine via the Mainz-based BioNTech, received the same per capita doses of the vaccine on the same day as citizens of Europe's poorest country, Bulgaria. Without any pre-existing legal requirement for doing so, the fear unleashed on the continent by the virus was leveraged to set aside localist interest and produce the emergence of a concrete universal: fair and equal access to vaccination in the face of a pandemic. Subsequent initiatives took the onus of institutionalizing and hence stabilizing this new right for the future.

Of course, while Europe may have been the world's most generous donor of vaccines, this ambitious equalization of benefits stopped at the borders of the Union. It was a *European* universal only. And yet, charity is not the point; scalability and prototyping are. Europe's actions prefigure a method for the emergence of a concrete universal for the planet. The planetary institution of such a concrete universal would have extended to the USA and Ghana the equalization that Europe made between Germany and Bulgaria.

A concrete universal is that which has been agreed to, that which has been universalized, that which has been collectively acquired until now. The European Union has a technical name for it: the *acquis communautaire*, that which the Community has acquired and has become a standard for all. We need to move from the *acquis communautaire* to the *acquis universel.* If we imagine the gradual emergence of specific and concrete covenants between the world's peoples, then the public goods, benefits, rights and security that they would extend to all would gradually construct the starting point of a novel conception of planetary citizenship.

Planetary citizenship

Kojin Karatani's celebrated *Structures of World History* presents an interesting analysis across the continuum of communities: tribal, imperial, national and, finally, at purely aspirational level, cosmopolitan.[8]

Karatani begins from a simple but radical proposal: human societies are shaped not only by modes of production, as Marx suggested, but by modes of exchange. He identifies three that recur across history. What he terms Mode A is reciprocity:

the network of gift and counter-gift that binds kinship groups and communities together, creating obligations of mutual care. Mode B is ruling and protection: the extraction of goods or labour by a ruling power, justified by its promise of order and defence, institutionalized in taxation and redistribution. Mode C is commodity exchange: the market logic of equivalence, where goods and labour are exchanged as if abstractly equal. These three modes, of course, never exist in isolation. Every society is a composite in which all three are entangled, even if one mode appears dominant. The nation-state, for instance, rests simultaneously on reciprocal bonds of citizenship (A), on state coercion and taxation (B), and on capitalist markets (C).

It is Karatani's speculative Mode D that is the most interesting for us. This would be a mode of association transcending the trinity of capital, nation and state and fostering an arrangement no longer determined by reciprocity, coercion or commodity exchange. Karatani suggests it would take the shape of a new cosmopolitanism, a form of association binding people as equals beyond borders. Yet he acknowledges that Mode D does not exist anywhere as a stable reality. At best, it flickers, à la Walter Benjamin, in fragmentary forms: in religious communities, cooperative movements or gestures of international solidarity. As such, Mode D remains a horizon, a regulative idea, more aspirational than realized.

Our account of concrete universality gives currency to Mode D. Rather than leaving it as an open wish, we can see it as arising wherever a singular act or principle becomes universally binding and institutionalized through practice. A situated universality emerges not as an abstract cosmopolitan law, but in specific enactments that bind everyone everywhere – on issues as diverse as artificial intelligence, nuclear regulation, health, mobility, education, culture, etc. Not cosmopolitanism as vague aspiration, but a new form of planetary citizenship as the fragile realization of universals that are enacted, translated and sustained as ontopoietic facts. We conceive *concrete cosmopolitanism* as the progressive construction of concrete universals that bind humanity on a narrow, albeit growing, but not totalizing set of issues.

Developing a web of concrete universal practices would gradually reinforce the feeling of planetary belonging, fostering a growing constituency for the continuation and acceleration of the process as thresholds are passed. A common humanity comes into being through its own habitual, repeated mobilization – it does not precede its own institution through practice, but comes into existence through it. At multiple stages, such accumulation of practices, habits, institutions, agreements and shared common sense reaches a threshold that transforms a singular, individualized habit into a self-aware, subject-defining commonality of purpose. A universal subject constituted by multiple universal objects.

The only path to concretizing such an aspiration is to become its interpreters.

I am a part of all I have met

> I am a part of all that I have met;
> Yet all experience is an arch wherethro'
> Gleams that untravell'd world whose margin fades
> For ever and forever when I move.

Where Jorge Luis Borges mourns the real tiger we may never reach, Alfred Lord Tennyson's poem 'Ulysses' reverses the perspective. Where, in Borges, the poet decries the golden cage that encloses us, making all our perceptions inescapably and merely *a part of us,* Tennyson sees the subjects leaning outwards from their individuality and becoming *a part of all* they cross on their voyage. This reversal is akin to the one we have attempted.

Where European universalism functioned by subsumption, absorbing all that it encountered as it travelled outwards from its place of origin, Tennyson reverses the approach: the traveller does not subsume the world, but is subsumed by it. Or, more accurately, self and world, community and universality, create one another and emerge through the encounter.

Where the logic of Being stood for a closed system, a revealed truth or an overarching way of life that is enveloped around the world like a constraining dress, Tennyson's stanza provides us with a different insight: the world that the traveller becomes a part of never ends; it has no closure, but expands as one moves through it, just like the horizon. The horizon is nothing but the horizon of a world, or the line that delimits it, changing location as that world transforms itself.

We have sketched a conception of universality that respects these two conditions. First, a universality that does not demand the world to conform to it, but, rather, one that gradually becomes itself a part of a world. Not a voracious worldview that ingests all that crosses its path and fixes it, but a vehicle, a travel or a process, allowing the successive creation of concrete universals that bind everyone everywhere.

Second, a universality not as a closed system, but as a voyage without end. A universality as a process that would yield concrete universals incessantly – producing, replacing, updating and renegotiating them. This is not a journey of discovery, with a total mapping of the land of universality as crowning success, but a travel of collective creation. It has no end: its margins fade for ever and forever when we move. And yet in that movement lies the secret to the construction of a planetary subjectivity – paraphrasing Nāgārjuna, there is a *goer* where there is a *going*.

The universal is a voyage and an *ethos*. And those engaged in the process of universalizing would be painstakingly looking for that which can bring us together, however modest it may appear, and try to institutionalize it. The party of concrete universalists would stand for the gradual development of a web of concrete and specific practices, policies and institutions of universal scope. They would relinquish any new grounding or ordering principle, while at the same time accepting that some things are at some time better than others for everyone everywhere. In so doing, they would plant the seeds for a common humanity to bloom.

This is a long-term process of creation that no single country, no single branch of knowledge, no enlightened mind and no single summit can define and resolve. It is a process that takes time. Between President Eisenhower's 1953 'Atom for Peace' speech and the actual entry into force of the treaty establishing the International Atomic Agency, nearly four years passed. Between the first speech by Arvid Pardo in 1967 and the establishment of the proposed United Nations Convention on the Law of the Sea, fifteen years passed. Between the first decision to create the Intergovernmental Panel on Climate Change and the adoption of the Paris Agreement, a whopping twenty-seven years went by. Concrete universality raises a demand to claim back duration, to think through the capacity to guide transformations over the long term and to imagine our agency in a process akin to geological sedimentation and formation.

This is a task for intellectuals and scientists the way Alexandre Kojève conceived of them: political individuals capable of bridging the search for the truth, the good and the beautiful. This is a task for philosophers the way Confucian, Daoist or Buddhist thought conceived of them: scholars who are monks who are government officials; thinkers who are doers. This is a task for artists, activists and creators understood as system designers who compose the conditions under which collective expression can occur. Where philosophy and politics become *poiesis*, then the poets of reality are the *interpres*, the individuals, collectives, natural and artificial agents capable of combining theoretical pursuit and practical engagement, not disclosing but dislocating the world and contributing to its incessant creative transformation.

Notes

Introduction: Of Nations and Truths

1 It is, of course, only following the social wars of the first century BC that the privileges of Roman citizenship would be expanded to the Italian peninsula, and only in AD 212 that Roman citizenship would be expanded to all inhabitants of the Empire with the Antonine Constitution.

2 Clifford Ando and Seth Richardson, eds., *Ancient States and Infrastructural Power: Europe, Asia, and America* (University of Pennsylvania Press, 2017).

3 As Hannah Arendt has argued, European empires, as the empires of nation-states, lacked the capacity of ruling over multiple peoples and states while respecting their diversity: 'Conquest as well as empire building had fallen into disrepute for very good reasons. They had been carried out successfully only by governments which, like the Roman Republic, were based primarily on law, so that conquest could be followed by integration of the most heterogeneous peoples by imposing upon them a common law. The nation-state, however, based upon a homogeneous population's active consent to its government ("*le plebiscite de tous les jours*"), lacked such a unifying principle and would, in the case of conquest, have to assimilate rather than to integrate, to enforce

consent rather than justice, that is, to degenerate into tyranny': *The Origins of Totalitarianism* (Harcourt, Brace & Company, 1951), 125. As Japanese philosopher Kojin Karatani summarizes it, 'imperialism means the domination of one nation by another nation-state in the absence of the governing principle of empire'. Karatani complements Arendt's reading with a duly materialist consideration: the total imposition of a way of life by European empires was due not merely to different forms of political governance, but to the different type of economy that each promoted. In the case of ancient empires, conquest resulted in the submission of the conquered population in exchange for military and economic security, leaving local customs and modes of existence mostly intact. Modern European imperialism, on the other hand, was based on the capitalist market, which dismantled existing tribal and agrarian communities, inserting them in a market economy. The uprooting of tradition suffered by colonized people is what triggers the need to 'imagine' the independent nation as the potential locus of equality. This is how imperialism ends up creating new nation-states without intending to. See Kojin Karatani, *The Structure of World History: From Modes of Production to Modes of Exchange*, trans. Michael K. Bourdaghs (Duke University Press, 2014), 225.

4 An arbitrary date for the emergence of modern imperialism may be found in the sixteenth-century moral and juridical controversy around the legitimacy of the Spanish conquest of Latin America and the coercion and enslavement of the native populations. Bartolomé de las Casas, a Spanish bishop notable for his blunt reporting of the depravity of Spanish rule, raised with Emperor Charles V and Pope Paul III the question of the inhuman treatment of native populations. Legally and ecclesiastically, he argued, native Americans deserved the respect owed to any human agent, and could not be enslaved, deprived of property rights or converted at gunpoint. While he never questioned the legitimacy of Spanish imperial rule, he argued for the type of respect for diversity expected in a multicultural empire. Las Casas had some

success. In 1537, Pope Paul III issued the bull *Sublimis Deus*, stating that native populations could not be enslaved and could be evangelized only by peaceful means. In 1543, Charles V passed the *Leyes Nuevas* (New Laws), which enacted a limited protection of native populations, taking up several of the proposals advanced by Las Casas. At about the same time, however, Spanish philosopher Juan Ginés de Sepúlveda advanced a very different view: native Americans, he argued, were 'barbarians, simple, unlettered, and uneducated, brutes totally incapable of learning anything but mechanical skills, full of vices, cruel and of a kind such that it is advisable they be governed by others'. In 1550, Emperor Charles V decided to convene a special juridical panel of the Consejo de Indias (Council of the Indies) to advise him about the merits of the controversy. The tribunal never gave a final verdict. But, with the accession to the throne of Charles V's son Philip, the arguments of Sepúlveda would become the dominant policy of the empire and the organizing principle of European expansion.

5 Antonio Gramsci, *Quaderni del carcere* (Einaudi, 1975), 1484; my emphasis. For an English rendition, see Antonio Gramsci, *Prison Notebooks*, vol. 3, ed. and trans. Joseph A. Buttigieg (Columbia University Press, 2007), 333–4.

6 Although Dipesh Chakrabarty does not raise Gramsci's misquotation, his analysis of situated Enlightenment emerges from similar considerations. See *Provincializing Europe: Postcolonial Thought and Historical Difference* (Princeton University Press, 2000).

7 Terms like 'Europe' and 'West' are of course undefinable. And while the former can at least refer to a geographical space, however shifting and open-ended, and to a millennial history of cultural and political entanglement, however porous, the latter is of much more recent and indefinite coinage. Yet, it is noticeable that the trend towards civilizational particularism seems to give greater definition to both terms. Europe tries to live up to its moment of geopolitical danger by erecting itself as *one*, a united civilization, and not the *universal* civilization. Something similar can be seen at play across the Atlantic: America-first is, ultimately, the

reverse-provincialization of the United States, as it attempts to construct itself as *one of many* and no longer the indispensable nation guiding the world. The West, too, acquires stronger civilizational overtones in opposition to the claims of the Rest, explaining the emergence of powerful tensions between competing visions of a liberal democratic or an illiberal Christian West.

8 When did the spectacles break? Already, modernist universalism has been being criticized for several decades, both from within Western societies and internationally. Postmodernism debunked and particularized all claims to objectivity; postcolonial and feminist critiques unmasked the partiality of the speaking someone who pretended to be everyone. And yet, until recently, such arguments were at the same time omnipresent in academia and much less tangible in the material life of Western populations. The rise of critical theory first and identity politics later brought home the internal critique: relations between genders and ethnicities began to be transformed not only in words, but also in deeds. The concurrent rise of non-Western actors compounded the blow, as the material transformation of the world economy lifted the curtain on the realized provincialization of the West. The period of Western-led globalization has marked not the end of history, but the end of Western centrality.

9 Souleymane Bachir Diagne, *Universaliser: L'humanité par les moyens d'humanité* (Albin Michel, 2024), 93–4.

10 Levinas puts it in the clearest terms: 'L'ethnographie la plus récente, la plus audacieuse et la plus influente, maintient sur le même plan les cultures multiples. L'œuvre politique de la décolonisation se trouve ainsi rattachée à une ontologie, à une pensée de l'être, interprétée à partir de la signification culturelle, multiple et multivoque. Et cette multivocité du sens de l'être – cette essentielle désorientation – est, peut-être, l'expression moderne de l'athéisme': Levinas, *Humanisme de l'autre homme*, quoted in Diagne, *Universaliser*, 97.

Ontopoiesis

1 Aristotle, *Metaphysics*, trans. W. D. Ross, in *The Complete Works of Aristotle*, ed. Jonathan Barnes, vol. 2 (Princeton University Press, 1984), 1003a21–22.

2 Aristotle, *Categories* 6a36–6b9, where Aristotle distinguishes what is said *pros ti* ('relative to another') from what is said *kath' hauto* ('in itself'), in *The Complete Works of Aristotle*, vol. 1, ed. Jonathan Barnes (Princeton University Press, 1984).

3 Plato, *Theaetetus* 176b, where the philosophical life is defined as 'becoming like god as far as possible' (*homoiōsis theōi kata to dynaton*), in *Plato: Complete Works*, ed. John M. Cooper (Hackett, 1997).

4 Aristotle, *Metaphysics*, vol. 2, 1006a11–25, 1006b7–9.

5 The figure of Friedrich Nietzsche represents the clearest example of the contortions of the modern mind as it tries to break free from this cage. Nietzsche's writing is aphoristic, self-contradictory and poetic, constantly recoiling in onto itself and stretching out again. Nietzsche must speak under erasure, facing at each turn the limitations of a language that cages him and returns him to the terrain of self-contradiction. Just as Latin American decolonial thinkers try to recuperate a space to speak and think outside the categories of Western modernity, so Nietzsche struggled with the difficulties of freeing up language from its millennial colonization by the Greek mind.

6 *A Treasury of Mahāyāna Sūtras*, trans. Garma C. C. Chang (Penn State University Press, 1983), 396.

7 For a fascinating run through the history of critique coupled with an impassionate call to step beyond it, see Laurent de Sutter, *Superweak* (Polity, 2026).

8 Jorge Luis Borges, 'The Other Tiger', trans. Alastair Reid, in *A Personal Anthology*, ed. Anthony Kerrigan (University of Texas Press, 1964).

9 Johann Wolfgang von Goethe, *Faust: A Tragedy, Part I*, trans. Walter Kaufmann (Anchor Books, 1961), 51.

10 Jure Simoniti has recently done a marvellous job in reconstructing the metaphysical core of postmetaphysics, and we can only point

the curious reader to his *Contingent Universality* (Bloomsbury Press, 2026).

11 Arguably the Mohists in the fifth century BCE did attempt to introduce the notion of a creator. It was, however, a short-lived parenthesis that would quickly be brushed aside and forgotten until the encounter with European metaphysics.

12 Roger T. Ames and David L. Hall, *Focusing the Familiar: A Translation and Philosophical Interpretation of the Zhongyong* (University of Hawai'i Press, 2001), 48.

13 In *Meno*, Plato would expand on this concept: 'True opinions, so long as they remain, are a fine thing and do all sorts of good, but they are not willing to remain for long, and they escape from a man's soul, so that they are not worth much until one ties them down by giving an account of the reason why. And that, Meno, is recollection, as we previously agreed. After they are tied down, in the first place they become knowledge, and then they remain in place. That is why knowledge is more valued than correct opinion, and knowledge differs from correct opinion in being tied down': 97e–98a, in *Plato: Complete Works*, ed. John M. Cooper.

14 'What encourages us within a Western metaphysical tradition to separate time and space is our inclination, inherited from the Greeks, to see things in the world as fixed in their formal aspect, and thus as bounded and limited. If, instead of giving ontological privilege to the formal aspect of phenomena, we were to regard them as having parity in their formal and changing aspects, we might be more like classical China in temporalizing them in light of their ceaseless transformation, and conceive of them more as "events" than as "things". In this processual worldview, each phenomenon is some unique current or impulse within a temporal flow. In fact, it is the pervasive and collective capacity of the events of the world to transform continuously that is the actual meaning of time': Roger T. Ames and David L. Hall, *Dao De Jing: A Philosophical Translation* (Ballantine Books, 2003), 28.

15 This is, incidentally, how Europe also thought of time and space before Newton. Time was understood as a measure of change: we

count days, seasons, swings of a pendulum; if nothing changes, there is no time to count. Space, likewise, was not an empty stage but a milieu of places (*topoi*): where a thing is defined by what surrounds it and not by coordinates in a homogeneous void. The pre-Newtonian picture was relational through and through: 'when' is tied to processes, and 'where' is tied to situational placement among things. The later Newtonian idea of a universal clock and of space as an empty container was a historical detour – one that has now come undone with the theories of general relativity and quantum mechanics. See, for instance, Carlo Rovelli, *The Order of Time* (Riverhead, 2018), chs. 1–2; *Reality Is Not What It Seems* (Riverhead, 2017), chs. 3–4.

16 On the recurring dismissal of Chinese philosophy in the Western canon, see G. W. F. Hegel's *Lectures on the History of Philosophy*, vol. 1, trans. E. S. Haldane and Frances H. Simson (University of Nebraska Press, 1995), 117–42, where he argues that Chinese thought is essentially practical and without true philosophy. Bertrand Russell likewise questioned whether Confucian thought amounted to philosophy; see *The Problem of China* (Allen & Unwin, 1922), 94–5.

17 Contrast this with Graham Harman's interpretation. Harman, the mind behind 'object-oriented ontology', sees philosophy as the great art of allusion to a real that cannot manifest itself. For him, too, 'things are events'. But an event is understood as an encounter or interaction between objects that does not fully reveal or exhaust their essence. According to his Heideggerian reading, objects are *withdrawn*, meaning that they possess an inner life or reality that remains hidden and cannot be entirely accessed or influenced by other objects, even when they interact. Objects interact while retaining an aspect of mystery or inaccessibility, emphasizing a world of discrete, independent entities whose depths cannot be wholly captured by their relations.

18 Quoted in Xiang Shuchen, *Chinese Cosmopolitanism: The History and Philosophy of an Idea* (Princeton University Press, 2023), 152–3.

19 Confucius, *The Analects of Confucius: A Philosophical Translation*, trans. Roger T. Ames and Henry Rosemont, Jr. (Ballantine Books, 1998), 2:14.

20 *Daodejing: A Philosophical Translation*, trans. Roger T. Ames and David L. Hall (Ballantine Books, 2003), Ch. 49; my emphasis.

21 The story is found in Chapter 2 of *Zhuangzi*, 'Discussion on making all things equal' (*Qi Wu Lun* 齐物论).

22 *Zhuangzi: A New Translation of the Sayings of Master Zhuang as Interpreted by Guo Xiang*, trans. Richard John Lynn (Columbia University Press, 2022), 34.

23 Confucius, *The Analects of Confucius*, 17:19.

24 François Jullien, *Il saggio è senza idee* (Einaudi, 2002), 8; my translation.

25 *Zhuangzi: A New Translation*, 55.

26 Ames and Hall, *Focusing the Familiar*, 40–5.

27 John Gray, *The New Leviathans: Thoughts After Liberalism* (London: Allen Lane, 2023), 119–20.

28 Martin Heidegger, *The Principle of Reason*, trans. Reginald Lilly (Indiana University Press, 1991), 36.

29 Aristotle's theory of the 'mean' posits that moral virtues are achieved by maintaining a balance between two extremes: one of excess and one of deficiency. Virtue, therefore, is a moderate state determined by reason as a prudent person would determine it. Courage is the mean between rashness and cowardice. The mean is relative to the individual and the specific circumstances, not an exact mathematical middle, and it calls on practical wisdom (*phronesis*) to discern the appropriate mean in any given situation. The Chinese conception, however, does without such binaries and a tempered *logos* of balance: under certain circumstances, it may be that that *one extreme* of the dichotomy is preferable.

30 The *Zhongyong* is one of the classical 'Four Books' of Confucianism, which collectively spell out its key philosophical and moral tenets. The others are the *Analects of Confucius*, the *Great Learning* and the *Mencius*.

31 Ames and Hall, *Focusing the Familiar*, 75–6.

32 Yamauchi Tokuryû, *Logos et Lemme* (CNRS Editions, 2020), 319.
33 Shuchen, *Chinese Cosmopolitanism*, 155.
34 Each of the two concepts presents a slightly different nuance of a similar overall disposition. *Gănyìng* means 'stimulus-response' or 'resonance', describing spontaneous interaction between different orders of reality – commonly between human ethical conduct and cosmic or natural phenomena. *Găntōng*, in contrast, emphasizes mutual resonance, penetration and a reciprocal spiritual or cognitive connection between beings or realms. While both terms articulate interconnectedness and resonance, *gănyìng* highlights cosmological responsiveness within a moral and natural order, whereas *găntōng* foregrounds mutual empathic communion and intuitive understanding between individuals or states of consciousness.
35 Ames and Hall (*Focusing the Familiar*) choose to translate the principle of '*cheng*' – the virtue associated with bringing things to consummation and usually translated as 'sincerity' – with the term 'creativity' precisely to underscore the active nature of the letting-be of harmony.
36 Heraclitus, Fragment B50 (DK), in G. S. Kirk, J. E. Raven and M. Schofield, *The Presocratic Philosophers*, 2nd ed. (Cambridge University Press, 1983), 187.
37 Reiner Schürmann, *The Philosophy of Nietzsche*, ed. Francesco Guercio (University of Chicago Press, 2020), 134.
38 David L. Hall and Roger T. Ames, 'Daoist Philosophy', *Routledge Encyclopedia of Philosophy* (Routledge, 1998), 7.
39 Byung-Chul Han, *Abwesen. Zur Kultur und Philosophie des Fernen Ostens* (Merve Verlag, 2007), 32.
40 For a short overview of the connections between Vedanta and Buddhist thought on this question, see Swami Sarvapriyananda, *Fullness & Emptiness: Vedanta and Buddhism* (Vedanta Society of New York, 2005).
41 Twentieth-century Sri Lankan Buddhist philosopher David J. Kalupahana, in his commentary on these verses, notes that '*ārtha* as well as *paramārtha* are truths (*satya*). The former is not presented as an un-truth (*a-satya*) in relation to the latter ... neither is

the former sublated by the latter': *Nāgārjuna: A Translation of his Mūlamādhyamakakārikā, with an Introductory Essay* (The Hokuseido Press, 1986), 96.

42 For a contemporary treatment, see Bing Song and Yiwen Zhan, eds., *Gongsheng Across Contexts: A Philosophy of Co-Becoming* (Palgrave Macmillan, 2024).

43 Tokuryū, *Logos et Lemme*, 143.

44 There is little surprise that the thought of Nāgārjuna appeals to several contemporary quantum physicists, such as Carlo Rovelli or Michel Bitbol. Physicist and philosopher Karen Barad, for instance, opens her ontology of quantum entanglements with a description that might just as well be speaking about Nāgārjuna's thought on co-dependence: 'To be entangled is not simply to be intertwined with another, as in the joining of separate entities, but to lack an independent, self-contained existence. Existence is not an individual affair. Individuals do not preexist their interactions; rather, individuals emerge through and as part of their entangled intra-relating': *Meeting the Universe Halfway* (Duke University Press, 2007), ix.

45 Aristotle, *Metaphysics*, vol. 2, 1007a20–30.

46 Zhao Tingyang, *The Existential Theory of Verbs* (Berggruen Press, forthcoming); quoted from unpublished manuscript.

47 Kant famously uses *antinomies*, or dilemmic contradictions, to show the limitations of pure reason. Post-Kantian philosophy would continuously reduce the space freed of contradiction until all thought becomes caged in self-referential representation.

48 Tokuryū, *Logos et Lemme*, 381.

49 Tokuryū, *Logos et Lemme*, 115.

50 Heraclitus, Fragment B90 (DK), in *Heraclitus: Fragments*, trans. T. M. Robinson (University of Toronto Press, 1987).

51 'The true world – we have abolished. What world has remained? The apparent one perhaps? But no! With the true world we have also abolished the apparent one.' Friedrich Nietzsche, 'How the 'real world' finally became a fable', in *Twilight of the Idols* (Oxford University Press, 2008).

52 See Barbara Cassin and Michel Narcy, *La Décision du sens: Le livre gamma de la métaphysique d'Aristote* (Vrin, 2000).

53 The theory of the Threefold Truth as formulated by Zhiyi (538–597 CE) and embodied in the Tiantai school of Buddhism clarifies the role of the Middle Way as a principle of mediation between being and emptiness and, at the theoretical level, the phenomenal and the ultimate.

54 A. A. Long and David N. Sedley, *The Hellenistic Philosophers*, vol. 1 (Cambridge University Press, 1987), p. 246, translating Aristocles in Eusebius, *Praeparatio Evangelica* 14.18.1–5; my emphasis.

55 Thomas McEvilley, *The Shape of Ancient Thought: Comparative Studies in Greek and Indian Philosophies* (Allworth Press, 2002).

56 Marcel Conche's reading places the accent precisely on this aspect: 'In Pyrrho's thought there is no separation between the subjective and the objective. Since appearances conceal no hidden depth . . . there is no "pole" capable of serving as object in relation to an opposing pole that would be the subject. Appearances are neither appearances-of nor appearances-for, but appearances in and of themselves': *Pyrrhon ou l'apparence*, 2nd ed. (Presses Universitaires de France, 1994), 51.

57 Quote in Conche, *Pyrrhon ou l'apparence*, 61.

58 Conche, *Pyrrhon ou l'apparence*; translation by the author.

59 Sextus Empiricus, *Outlines of Pyrrhonism*, trans. R.G. Barry (Harvard University Press, 1933, reprinted 2000), Book I, ch. 14, §§ 135–6. Contrast phenomena with Zeno's concept of true impressions, which would anchor European thought on the course and the curse of representationalism: 'An impression is an imprint on the soul: that which proceeds from a real object, conforms to that object, and is stamped and sealed upon the mind': Diogenes Laërtius, *Lives of the Eminent Philosophers*, trans. R.D. Hicks (Harvard University Press, 1925), 184–5, §45.

60 On African philosophies and their relation to relationality and process, see Souleymane Bachir Diagne, *African Art as Philosophy: Senghor, Bergson and the Idea of Negritude* (Seagull Books, 2011),

which reads Negritude as a processual philosophy of rhythm and relation; Achille Mbembe, *On the Postcolony* (University of California Press, 2001), which gestures to cyclical and processual African temporalities; Mogobe B. Ramose, *African Philosophy Through Ubuntu* (Mond Books, 1999), a major work articulating ubuntu as being-in-relation; and Kwasi Wiredu, *Cultural Universals and Particulars: An African Perspective* (Indiana University Press, 1996), which explores relational personhood and communal ontology.

61 Among the vast literature covering Indigenous relational and processual cosmology, see John Borrows, *Drawing Out Law: A Spirit's Guide* (University of Toronto Press, 2010), which reimagines law as a dynamic relational practice; Vine Deloria Jr., *God Is Red: A Native View of Religion* (Fulcrum Publishing, 1992), contrasting Indigenous relational cosmologies with Western substance metaphysics; Marisol de la Cadena, *Earth Beings: Ecologies of Practice across Andean World*s (Duke University Press, 2015), showing Andean earth beings as participants in relational worlds; and Eduardo Viveiros de Castro, *Cannibal Metaphysics*, trans. Peter Skafish (Univocal, 2014), which develops Amazonian perspectivism as a philosophy of becoming.

62 Arturo Escobar, *Pluriversal Politics: The Real and the Possible*, trans. David Frye (Duke University Press, 2020), 14.

63 Niels Bohr, 'Discussion with Einstein on epistemological problems in atomic physics', in *Albert Einstein: Philosopher–Scientist*, ed. Paul Arthur Schilpp (Open Court, 1949), 210.

64 Notably, Karen Barad, *Meeting the Universe Halfway: Quantum Physics and the Entanglement of Matter and Meaning* (Duke University Press, 2007).

65 An example of a radicalization of epistemic and subjectivist approaches to quantum reality is offered by twenty-first-century QBism, which emphasizes that quantum states represent subjective degrees of belief about experiences. Quantum probabilities express an agent's expectations regarding their personal interactions with nature. QBism asserts we can never step outside our

experiences but must navigate a reality continually co-constructed through interaction, perception and probabilistic judgement with and for the subject.

66 Carlo Rovelli, *Helgoland: Making Sense of the Quantum Revolution*, trans. Erica Segre and Simon Carnell (Riverhead Books, 2021), 77.

67 For instance, the experimental confirmation of Bell's Theorem, a key empirical test of a thought experiment of quantum theory, disproves the classical notion of independently existing entities with intrinsic properties. It shows that either objects do not possess definite properties prior to observation, or that they can instantaneously influence one another across spatial distance – or both. In either case, what the experiments disprove is the idea of individual objects as self-contained, ontologically autonomous units with a specific set of properties. See Adam Becker, *What Is Real? The Unfinished Quest for the Meaning of Quantum Physics* (Basic Books, 2018). Another empirical test from the year 2000 – the quantum eraser experiment – seems to confirm there is no magical action at distance but, rather, objects and agencies of observation are inseparable parts of a single phenomenon.

68 'A phenomenon is a specific intra-action of an "object" and the "measuring agencies"; the object and the measuring agencies emerge from, rather than precede, the intra-action that produces them. Crucially, then, we should understand phenomena not as objects-in-themselves or as perceived objects (in the Kantian or phenomenological sense), but as specific intra-actions. Because the basis of this ontology is a fundamental inseparability, it cuts across any Kantian noumena–phenomena distinction: there are no determinately bounded or propertied entities existing "behind" or as the causes of phenomena': Barad, *Meeting the Universe Halfway*, 139.

69 Carlo Rovelli, 'Relational quantum mechanics', *International Journal of Theoretical Physics* 35, no. 8 (1996), 1637–78.

70 Carlo Rovelli, 'An argument against the realistic interpretation of the wave function', *Foundations of Physics* 46, no. 10 (2016), 1230–1.

71 Carlo Rovelli, 'Space is blue and birds fly through it', *Philosophical Transactions of the Royal Society* 376, no. 2123 (2018), 20170312: https://doi.org/10.1098/rsta.2017.0312.

72 G. W. F. Hegel, *Phenomenology of Spirit*, trans. A. V. Miller (Oxford University Press, 1977), 21.

73 Rovelli, 'Relational quantum mechanics', 1641. Thomas Hertog makes a similar point, see his *On the Origin of Time* (Penguin, 2023).

74 Bas C. van Fraassen, 'Rovelli's world', *Foundations of Physics* 40, no. 4 (2010), 390–417, esp. p. 396.

75 This point is explicitly raised by Mauro Dorato in connection to Carlo Rovelli's relational quantum mechanics. See Dorato, Mauro. 'Bohr meets Rovelli: A dispositionalist account of the quantum limits of knowledge', *Quantum Studies: Mathematics and Foundations* 7 (2020), 233–45, esp. p. 245.

76 Carlo Rovelli, 'Space is blue and birds fly through it', *Philosophical Transactions of the Royal Society* 376, no. 2123 (2018), 20170312. https://doi.org/10.1098/rsta.2017.0312.

77 This recalls the characterization of *Dao* in the *Daodejing*: 'The ecology of Dao gives rise to one as continuity' (*Daodejing*, 42). Since *dao* is an unbounded and non-totalizable totality of all that is, it cannot be predicated as 'one' in the sense of a discrete entity, but since it is construed from the perspective of each insistent particular, it cannot be differentiated as this field as opposed to that.

78 Heidegger interprets the image of Time as a child at play not as a symbol of arbitrariness, but as an expression of the primordial movement of Being. Play, for Heidegger, is not lawless but unfolds according to a deeper *logos* – a gathering that holds opposites in tension without reducing them to unity. The becoming of world-time is thus playful yet ordered, not governed by rational necessity but by the self-disclosing rhythm of Being itself. See his *Introduction to Metaphysics*, trans. Gregory Fried and Richard Polt (Yale University Press, 2000), 44–8.

79 Conche, *Pyrrhon ou l'apparence*, ch. XVI, esp. the discussion distinguishing a 'philosophie mobiliste' from 'philosophies du logos';

cf. Sextus Empiricus, *Outlines of Pyrrhonism*, trans. R. G. Bury, in *Sextus Empiricus*, vol. 1, Loeb Classical Library (Harvard University Press, 1933), §§210–12, on Aenesidemus and the alleged path from Pyrrhonism to Heraclitus.

80 Slavoj Žižek, *Quantum Time*, (Bloomsbury Academic, 2025).

81 Aristotle, *Metaphysics*, vol. 2, 1026a 7–33.

82 Roger T. Ames, *Human Becomings* (State University of New York Press, 2021), 218.

83 Tingyang, *The Existential Theory of Verbs.*

84 Lynn Margulis, *Symbiosis in Cell Evolution* (W. H. Freeman, 1981).

85 Emanuele Coccia, *Metamorphoses* (Polity, 2021).

86 James Lovelock, *Gaia: A New Look at Life on Earth* (Oxford University Press, 1979); *The Ages of Gaia: A Biography of Our Living Earth* (Oxford University Press, 1995).

87 Bruno Latour, *Facing Gaia: Eight Lectures on the New Climatic Regime*, trans. Catherine Porter (Polity, 2017).

88 Catherine Malabou, *Morphing Intelligence: From IQ Measurement to Artificial Brains*, trans. Carolyn Shread (Columbia University Press, 2021), 78.

Politics as First Philosophy

1 Janna Tay, 'A phenomenology of protocols', in *Protocol Reader: Summer of Protocols* (Ethereum Foundation, 2023). https://summerofprotocols.com/research/a-phenomenology-of-protocols.

2 For an overview of protocol art, see: Primavera De Filippi, 'Protocolism: Shifting paradigms in art and copyright', in Holly Herndon and Mathew Dryhurst, *All Media is Training Data*, ed. Eva Jäger and Caroline Busta (Verlag der Buchhandlung Walther, 2024); Botao Amber Hu, 'Protocol as poetry: Case study of Pak's smart contract-based protocol arts', *arXiv* (2025), https://arxiv.org/abs/2505.12393; *Protocol Reader: Summer of Protocols* (2023).

3 Primavera De Filippi and Aaron Wright, *Blockchain and the Law: The Rule of Code* (Harvard University Press, 2018).

4 Alexander R. Galloway, *Protocol: How Control Exists after Decentralization* (MIT Press, 2004), 7.

5 Sun Ge and Naoki Sakai, *Universality and Particularity: What Is Asianness?* (Archive Books, 2022).

6 Sun Ge's empirical reasoning could be associated with Donna Haraway's situated objectivity: both reject detached, universal abstraction in favour of contextual, embodied, accountable knowledge production. See Haraway's influential essay 'Situated knowledges: The science question in feminism and the privilege of partial perspective', *Feminist Studies* 14, no. 3 (1988), 575–99.

7 And even in controlled scientific experiments, the apparatus is still material, the observer is a human being belonging to the institution of science; the context then easily broadens out of its supposedly controlled scale.

8 Bruno Latour's account of truth as the stabilization of chains of reference becomes newly relevant here: a statement is true to the extent that it holds together across the operations or protocols that sustain it; see *An Inquiry into Modes of Existence* (Harvard University Press, 2012).

9 Michel Foucault, 'The confession of the flesh', in *Power/Knowledge: Selected Interviews and Other Writings, 1972–1977*, ed. Colin Gordon (Pantheon Books, 1980), 194.

10 Alexander R. Galloway, *Protocol: How Control Exists after Decentralization* (MIT Press, 2004), 7.

11 The conceptual pairing of form (or substance) and function is known in Chinese philosophy as *ti-yong* 体用. While the terms appear in classical commentaries such as Wang Bi's Laozi zhu, the fully developed doctrine – holding that form and function are 'mutually implicating moments of one process' – is most closely associated with the neo-Confucian synthesis of Zhu Xi (1130–1200). For an overview of the historical development of the concept from cosmology to ontology, see Qi Feng and Weiping Chen, *A Concise History of Chinese Philosophy* (Springer, 2023), Ch. 6.

12 See, among a wide literature, Merlin Sheldrake, *Entangled Life: How Fungi Make Our Worlds, Change Our Minds and Shape Our Futures* (Bodley Head, 2020); Michael Marder, *Plant-Thinking: A Philosophy of Vegetal Life* (Columbia University Press, 2013).

13 Carlo Rovelli, 'Relational quantum mechanics', *International Journal of Theoretical Physics* 35, no. 8 (1996), 1637–78; 'Space is blue and birds fly through it', *Philosophical Transactions of the Royal Society* 376, no. 2123 (2018), 20170312: https://doi.org/10.1098/rsta.2017.0312.

14 Benoît B. Mandelbrot, 'How long is the coast of Britain? Statistical self-similarity and fractional dimension', *Science* 156, no. 3775 (1967), 636–8.

15 Hartmut Rosa, *Resonance*, trans. James C. Wagner (Polity, 2019), 84.

16 Cornelius Castoriadis differentiates between constitutive and institutive power to elucidate how societies create and maintain themselves. Constitutive power refers to the explicit and formalized ability to establish and legitimize political structures, institutions, laws and norms. It corresponds to organized mechanisms, such as constitutions or foundational legal frameworks, that define and stabilize society. Institutive power, by contrast, denotes the deeper, creative and often unconscious force of societal self-creation, or imaginary institution. It embodies society's capacity to produce new meanings, values, social roles and forms of existence prior to, or beneath, explicit institutionalization.

17 Pierre Bourdieu's notion of *habitus* describes how social structures inscribe themselves in bodies, sedimenting as dispositions that generate practices and perceptions. The world endures because it is reproduced in our postures, our tastes, our accents, our ways of moving without thought. To walk or to greet in a certain way is already to perform one's place in a field of relations. Yet, like Confucian ritual, *habitus* is never immutable: it adapts as contexts change, layering new dispositions over old ones. For Bourdieu, habit is not essence but history carried in the body, the continual re-enactment of a social order. Alva Noë pushes this insight further still, arguing that life and mind are not hidden inside us but enacted in our relations with the world. To perceive is not to receive images but to act: to reach, to move, to attune oneself in practice. Perception is enactive and relational, culture

is a process of entanglement. See Pierre Bourdieu, *Outline of a Theory of Practice* (Cambridge University Press, 1977); Alva Noë, *Entanglement* (Princeton University Press, 2023).

18 *A New Translation of the Sayings of Master Zhuang as Interpreted by Guo Xiang*, trans. Richard John Lynn (Columbia University Press, 2022). The line 'Life is in mutual forgetting; it will have no end' occurs in Chapter 6, 'The Great Ancestral Teacher', where Confucius praises Yan Hui's practice of 'sitting in forgetfulness'. The phrase conveys the Daoist teaching that when self and world 'forget' one another, bounded individuality dissolves into the endless, transformative flow of the Dao.

19 Roger T. Ames and David L. Hall, *Focusing the Familiar: A Translation and Philosophical Interpretation of the Zhongyong* (University of Hawai'i Press, 2001), 21.

20 Gary G. Hamilton and Wang Zheng Wang, ed. and trans., *From the Soil: The Foundations of Chinese Society: A Translation of Fei Xiaotong's Xiangtu Zhongguo* (University of California Press, 1992).

21 For Carl Schmitt, law is never an abstract system of rules that floats above social life. 'Every law', he writes, 'is bound to a concrete order.' Within a state, such order is supplied by sovereignty and law is possible only where a sovereign exists to sustain it. Between states, no overarching sovereign stands above them; there is no concrete order to ground universal legal norms. This is then the terrain where the friend–enemy distinction remains primary: where no sovereign order exists, politics dominates, and law becomes subordinate to force. See Carl Schmitt, *The Nomos of the Earth in the International Law of the Jus Publicum Europaeum*, trans. G. L. Ulmen (Telos Press, 2003), 67.

22 Tristan Garcia, 'Hémisphères', in *7* (Paris: Gallimard, 2015), 311.

23 The promise and danger of *ontopoiesis* is spelled out clearly towards the end of Laurent de Sutter's *Superweak* (Polity, 2026): 'Let us repeat it: all is permitted, all is possible, everything exists, nothing has a reason, everyone is always wrong, everything is yet to be done, we know only what we do not know, the only thing that

matters is what comes to pass, the world is its own metamorphosis – and screw those who say otherwise' (p. 220).

24 Michel Foucault, 'What is Enlightenment?', in Paul Rabinow, ed., *The Foucault Reader* (Pantheon Books, 1984), 42.

25 Several authors, including Foucault himself, have drawn out this point, including Marina Garcés, *New Radical Enlightenment: Philosophy for a Common World* (Verso, 2024).

26 Foucault, 'What is Enlightenment?', 42.

27 Ibid., 45.

28 Ibid., 46.

29 A way of seeing, of course, is not merely perceptive but grounded in a myriad of material and historical conditions of possibility. The same is true in science: a particle accelerator, the scientific community utilizing it, and the institutions enabling it are all grounded in materiality and in history.

30 Confucius, *The Analects of Confucius: A Philosophical Translation*, trans. Roger T. Ames and Henry Rosemont, Jr. (Ballantine Books, 1998), 189.

31 Mohandas K. Gandhi, *An Autobiography: The Story of My Experiments with Truth*, trans. Mahadev Desai (Beacon Press, 1993), xiii.

32 See Michael Levin, 'Technological approach to mind everywhere: An experimentally-grounded framework for understanding diverse bodies and minds', *Frontiers in Systems Neuroscience* 16 (2022): 3–5; Alexis Pietak and Michael Levin, 'Harnessing the analog computing power of regulatory networks with the Regulatory Network Machine', *iScience* (2024), https://doi.org/10.31219/osf.io/tb5ys.

33 The mere presence of an ethos of universality can be creative or formative even when it fails to shy away from concretely realizing contextual universals. The Paris climate agreement, for instance, rests not on a single law binding all nations equally, but on a patchwork of nationally determined contributions that are pledged, revised and peer-reviewed. As Anne-Marie Slaughter argues, what appears as a weakness is in reality a strength: the treaty does not impose any one universal obligation on all, but

a shared orientation – keeping global warming 'well below' two degrees. The parties are then encouraged to submit increasingly stringent revisions of their so-called Intended Nationally Determined Contributions, based on their own judgement. See Anne-Marie Slaughter, 'The Paris approach to global governance', Project Syndicate, 28 December 2015, https://www.project-syndicate.org/commentary/paris-agreement-model-for-global-governance-by-anne-marie-slaughter-2015-12.

34 G. W. F. Hegel, *Science of Logic*, trans. A. V. Miller (Allen & Unwin, 1969).

35 Catherine Malabou, *The Future of Hegel: Plasticity, Temporality, and Dialectic* (Routledge, 2005). Malabou emphasizes how the universal is plastic, unfolding through historical mediations, though still underwritten by a logic of necessity in Hegel.

36 Martin Heidegger, *Identity and Difference*, trans. Joan Stambaugh (Harper & Row, 1969), 54–65.

37 Alexandre Kojève, *Sofia* (unpublished manuscript), 128, quoted in Boris Groys, *Alexandre Kojève: An Intellectual Biography* (Verso, 2025), 60.

38 The flattening of the human/natural distinction is of course a monumental gesture that challenges the very foundations of Kojevian/Hegelian thought, whereby humans are distinct from the natural world precisely because of their ability to renounce their animality, or the constraints of desires and the absolute primacy of the protection of life, and this notably by their ability to desire death, whether by committing suicide or by being willing to endanger their own survival. Readiness to die, in fact, is for Hegel what first separates masters from slaves.

39 Alfred North Whitehead, *Dialogues of Alfred North Whitehead* (David R. Godine, 2001), 363. This is of course a point pressed by Quentin Meillassoux in *After Finitude* (Polity, 2009).

40 Armen Avanessian, *Future Metaphysics* (Polity, 2020), 36.

41 Groys, *Alexandre Kojève*.

42 Wang Yangming, *Chuanxilu* 傳習錄 ('Instructions for practical living') sec. 5, trans. Wing-tsit Chan (Columbia University Press,

1963), 23. Wang's collapse of the distinction between cognition and action represents a specific ethical application of the broader *ti-yong* (form/function) paradigm discussed earlier. For Wang, knowledge (*zhi*) is the 'substance' (*ti*), and action (*xing*) is the 'function' (*yong*); the two are not separate stages but 'mutually implicating moments of one process'. On this reading of Wang's metaphysics, see Warren G. Frisina, *The Unity of Knowledge and Action: Toward a Nonrepresentational Theory of Knowledge* (SUNY Press, 2002), esp. Ch. 3, 'Wang Yangming and the Overcoming of the Inner-Outer Dichotomy.'

43 De Sutter, *Superweak*, 179.

44 Foucault, 'What is Enlightenment?', 46.

45 Michel Foucault, 'Truth and power', in *Power/Knowledge: Selected Interviews and Other Writings, 1972–1977*, ed. Colin Gordon (New York: Pantheon Books, 1980), 126.

46 Bruno Latour, *Reassembling the Social: An Introduction to Actor-Network-Theory* (Oxford University Press, 2005), esp. 63–5, where he argues for methodological symmetry among human and non-human actors. Also see Manuel DeLanda, *A New Philosophy of Society: Assemblage Theory and Social Complexity* (Continuum, 2006), which develops an ontology of assemblages where wholes and parts are treated without hierarchical reduction; Graham Harman, *The Quadruple Object* (Zero Books, 2011), which articulates object-oriented ontology as a flat field where objects withdraw from access yet remain equally real; and Tristan Garcia, *Form and Object: A Treatise on Things*, trans. Mark Allan Ohm and Jon Cogburn (Edinburgh University Press, 2014), which proposes a universal metaphysics where everything, regardless of scale or status, is treated symmetrically.

47 Among a rich and diverse set of books: Enrique Dussel, *The Invention of the Americas: Eclipse of 'the Other' and the Myth of Modernity*, trans. Michael D. Barber (Continuum, 1995), which critiques the Eurocentric 'myth of modernity' and opens the way for alternative universalities grounded in the experiences of the colonized; Arturo Escobar, *Pluriversal Politics: The Real and the*

Possible (Duke University Press, 2020), which explicitly theorizes the pluriverse as a framework for decolonial politics and ecological alternatives; Walter D. Mignolo, *The Darker Side of Western Modernity: Global Futures, Decolonial Options* (Duke University Press, 2011), which frames pluriversality as a decolonial response to the global dominance of Western universality.

48 This is a more general point on the question of rights and covenants, where the effect is not merely in the practical instantiation but in the ethos behind it. The Geneva Conventions of 1949, for instance, made the deliberate targeting of civilian populations illegal. They were drafted in response to the horrors of the Second World War and have been ratified by every country in the world. Again, their importance is not merely to stamp out violence against civilians: it is to push anyone engaging in it outside the world.

49 Michel de Montaigne, *The Essays*, Book I, Chapter 57 ('Of Age'), trans. John Florio (1603).

50 Barbara Cassin, *Sophistical Practice: Toward a Consistent Relativism* (Fordham University Press, 2014), xiv. Cassin repudiates the modern fixation on absolute Truth and proposes instead 'truth for, and enough of the truth for there to be a community', signifying a pragmatic, relational basis for communal coherence.

51 Ikhwān al-Safā' (Brethren of Purity), *The Case of the Animals versus Man Before the King of the Jinn: A Translation from the Epistles of the Brethren of Purity*, trans. Lenn E. Goodman and Richard McGregor (Oxford University Press, 2012).

52 *A New Translation of the Sayings of Master Zhuang*, trans. Lynn, 240. While there are exceptions – for instance, in the thought of Ming Dynasty Neo-Confucian philosopher Wang Yangming 王阳明 (1472–1529), who tried to expand humanity's moral obligation to animals, trees and stones – the Daoists generally condemned Confucians for remaining focused exclusively on the sociopolitical and ultimately human reality, and in doing so failing to integrate in the harmony of the world. Daoists insisted that resonance had to be opened up from the sociopolitical to

the cosmic order, from the human to the natural, recognizing the small part that humans play in the wider composition of the world.

53 Bruno Latour, for instance, argues that to 'limit the discussion to humans, their interest, their subjectivities, and their rights, will appear as strange a few years from now as having denied the right to vote of slaves, poor people, or women.' See *Politics of Nature: How to Bring the Sciences into Democracy*, trans. Catherine Porter (Harvard University Press, 2004), 69. As Nils Gilman writes, 'appreciating the condition of planetarity means rejecting the Aristotelian tradition that claims only humans (can) engage in politics . . . We need to imagine a new form of constitutionalism (or perhaps post-constitutionalism) that reflects our post-individualist, multispecies ontological reality.' See Jonathan S. Blake and Nils Gilman, *Children of a Modest Star: Planetary Thinking for an Age of Crises* (Stanford University Press, 2024).

54 In the American pragmatist tradition most recently updated by Richard Rorty, the concept of 'truth' inhabits a comparable predicament: 'If I am right that the only indispensable function of the word "true" (or any other indefinable normative term, such as "good" or "right") is to caution, to warn against danger by making gestures toward unpredictable situations (future audiences, future moral dilemmas, etc.), then it does not make much sense to ask whether or not justification leads to truth. Justification to more and more audiences leads to less and less danger of rebuttal, and thus to less and less need for caution.' See Rorty, *Pragmatism as Anti-Authoritarianism* (Harvard University Press, 2021), 63.

55 Slavoj Žižek, *For a Quantum Theory of History* (Berggruen Press, 2025).

56 Nadia Yala Kisukidi, 'L'universel dans la brousse', *Esprit*, no. 1 (janvier–février 2020), 47–59. In a similar vein, see also Souleymane Bachir Diagne, *Les Universels du Louvre* (Albin Michel, 2025).

57 See Lorenzo Marsili and Hans Ulrich Obrist, *What Is Universalism?* (Berggruen Press, 2026).

58 Wang Hui, *The Rise of Modern Chinese Thought* (Harvard University Press, 2023), 759.

59 Wang Hui, *The Rise of Modern Chinese Thought*, 773.

60 Rorty, *Pragmatism as Anti-Authoritarianism*, 17.

61 Sovereignty, in Hobbes's bleak recounting of the state of nature, emerges in one of two ways: through coercion or by agreement, that is, through a war of conquest or through the voluntary decision of an assembly of individuals. In the former case, Hobbes spoke of a commonwealth by acquisition, in the latter, by institution. Similarly, universals may emerge through an original imposition or a collective deliberation, but they nevertheless hold only for as long as they are accepted and recognised as such. Does this mean we put violence on a par with persuasion? Were North Korea to conquer the whole world and impose its doctrinal political system and culture – would those then be universal in the way we have described them? Yes. To the extent that there remained an insignificant space of contestation, the whims of a North Korean planetary dictator would appear to be universal whims. Is this really so frightening? An implausible planetary dictatorship without significant contestation would have a monopoly of universality, for as long as it did – that is to say, for as long it did not raise contestation and start to crack internally or externally because of its contradictions, or meet an alien species, or be confronted with the penchant for liberal democracy of the algorithmic singularity. Ultimately, even if a planetary dictatorship has no election cycles, reality, understood as time, does. This, incidentally, provides the greatest validation for opposition, resistance and political investment. The existence of an opposition factually removes universality from the incumbent power. In doing so, the emergence of an opposition shapes the universal, transforms it, marks its partial defeat even as it still yields to its command.

Coda: Universality as Method

1 Frederick Cooper, *Citizenship, Inequality, and Difference: Historical Perspectives* (Princeton University Press, 2018), 47.

2 Frederick Cooper, *Citizenship between Empire and Nation: Remaking France and French Africa, 1945–1960* (Princeton University Press, 2014).
3 Emmanuel Carrère, *Uchronie* (Éditions P.O.L, 1975). Carrère's first book is a study of counterfactual history – 'what if' scenarios that imagine alternative historical outcomes – an inquiry into the philosophical and narrative possibilities of history's contingency.
4 Quoted in Souleymane Bachir Diagne, *Universaliser: L'humanité par les moyens d'humanité* (Albin Michel, 2024), 53.
5 Diagne, *Universaliser*, 54.
6 Alexandre Kojève, 'Outline of a doctrine of French policy' (27 August 1945), trans. Erik de Vries, *Policy Review* 126 (August–September 2004), 3–40.
7 Mark S. Granovetter, 'The strength of weak ties: A network theory revisited', *Sociological Theory* 1 (1983), 201–33.
8 Kojin Karatani, *The Structure of World History: From Modes of Production to Modes of Exchange*, trans. Michael K. Bourdaghs (Duke University Press, 2014).

